A New Nation Inside of a Nation:

The Age of Technology and Black Dollar

Daniel Q. Easterly

ISBN: 9798870347448

Imprint: Independently published

Table of Contents

Preface

In the vast tapestry of history, threads of hope, resilience, and progress have woven together the story of the Black community in America. It's a narrative that stretches across centuries, from the darkest days of slavery to the dawn of the digital age. This book, "A New Nation inside of a Nation – The Age of the Black Dollar," is a tapestry of its own, tracing the evolution of the Black Dollar and the transformative power it holds.

As we embark on this journey, we must first acknowledge the indomitable spirit of those who have come before us – leaders like Martin Luther King Jr., Marcus Garvey, Malcolm X, and W.E.B. Du Bois. Their ideals laid the foundation for economic justice, self-reliance, and the fight against double consciousness. Their legacy continues to inspire and guide us.

The digital age has ushered in new paradigms, and this book delves into the intersection of technology and Black empowerment. We explore how the Black Panthers' legacy has evolved, the impact of desegregation, and the ongoing struggle for economic justice. We also venture into the realm of digital real estate, smart contracts, and the crypto revolution, uncovering opportunities for Black economic empowerment in the digital era.

Bridging two worlds – America and Africa – becomes a focal point as we examine the historical legacy of slavery, discuss socioeconomic unity, and explore collaborative economic strategies between continents. This journey reflects on the past while envisioning a future of strengthened relations and mutual progress.

Yet, challenges persist on the horizon. We confront mass incarceration, the complexities of the cannabis industry, the scars of redlining, and the pressing need to reform policing in Black communities. These challenges serve as a reminder that our journey towards empowerment is not without obstacles.

In the digital age, opportunities abound.

We probe into the collaborative potential between Africa and African Americans, explore the transformation of asset ownership, and emphasize the significance of smart contracts and NFTs in shaping the future of wealth. Access to digital wealth is within reach, and we must seize it.

As we conclude this narrative, we summarize the remarkable journey we have embarked upon – from historical ideologies to future prospects. We underscore the importance of a unified approach to economic empowerment and extend a call to action to the Black community. The potential of a new nation within a nation is ours to embrace.

Lastly, we explore the affiliations and partnerships that are shaping the future. "40'aces," an app developed by the author, and "WeCannBe," a company dedicated to reimagining Black enterprises, serve as beacons of hope and innovation.

This book is more than a collection of words; it is a testament to the enduring spirit of the Black community and the boundless potential for economic empowerment. It is a call to envision a decentralized destiny – a future where the Black Dollar thrives, igniting a new era of progress and unity.

Join us on this journey as we explore the Age of the Black Dollar – a journey that has the power to shape our collective future.

With hope and determination,

Daniel

Journey of a Renaissance Man: From the Fields to Silicon Valley

Born in Kansas City and raised in Detroit, my life has been a journey marked by movement and change, shaped significantly by my involvement in football and my parents' influence. This nomadic lifestyle instilled in me an adaptability and resilience that would later become instrumental in my career.

My academic journey began at the University of Missouri, where I pursued an undergraduate degree in Communications. Here, football was more than just a sport; it was a discipline that taught me about teamwork, leadership, and the importance of strategy. Balancing academics and athletics was challenging, but it laid the groundwork for my multifaceted career path.

After my undergraduate studies, I continued my education at Tennessee State University, where I worked towards a Master's degree in Business. This period was a time of significant growth, both intellectually and personally. It was here that I truly embraced my identity as a Renaissance man: an individual with diverse interests and talents. I delved into technology, cybersecurity, and art, while also exploring my entrepreneurial spirit in investing and real estate. My time as an athlete further honed my skills in discipline and focus, and I began to emerge as a scholar and public speaker.

These experiences were the bedrock upon which my professional journey was built. However, like many stories of success, mine was not without its setbacks. After university, I found myself navigating the dynamic and often unpredictable world of technology and fashion. My career path took unexpected turns, leading me through various roles and experiences. I was part of three different tech startups, each teaching me invaluable lessons about the industry, innovation, and the importance of agility in business.

However, the most pivotal moment in my journey came when I was working for a healthcare company. The company underwent a buyout, resulting in mass layoffs, and I found myself without a job. This setback, though disheartening, did not dampen my spirit. Instead, it propelled me into a period of introspection and reevaluation of my career goals.

During this transitional phase, I took up driving for Lyft. This job, seemingly a detour from my professional path, turned out to be a serendipitous stepping stone. As I navigated the streets, ferrying passengers to their destinations, I stumbled upon a tech company named Intuit. The sight of its basketball and volleyball courts and the vibrant atmosphere around its campus intrigued me. Unbeknownst to me at the time, this discovery would mark the beginning of a remarkable new chapter in my life.

Curiosity got the better of me that day as I observed Intuit's lively campus. With my resume conveniently in my car, I made an impulsive decision to stop and explore what this unknown company had to offer. This spur-of-the-moment choice was about to open a new doorway in my career.

As I walked towards the building, the importance of first impressions dawned on me. I quickly donned my suit jacket, transforming from a Lyft driver into a potential job candidate within moments. Approaching the security guard with confidence, I was asked the purpose of my visit. Without a clear plan, I blurted out that I was there for an interview. The guard, understandably, inquired about the person I was supposed to meet. Thinking on my feet, I randomly selected an executive named Ryan from the company's LinkedIn page.

The guard directed me to wait while he verified my supposed interview. During this brief pause, I asked to use the restroom. This request inadvertently granted me a broader access to the building. As I left the restroom, a bold idea struck me. Instead of returning to the lobby, I ventured into the heart of the building, immersing myself in the environment of Intuit.

The building was impressive, a hub of innovation and collaboration. As I walked around, introducing myself to various employees, I realized how fortunate I was to have my resume and suit jacket with me. My unplanned tour led to an unexpected encounter with Ryan, the executive I had named earlier. He was looking for me, curious about the unexpected visitor who had an 'interview' with him.

In that moment, I handed Ryan my resume, seizing the opportunity to make a memorable impression. This chance encounter proved fortuitous when, two weeks later, Ryan called me with a job offer. Three months after our initial meeting, I officially joined Intuit. Our conversation as we walked out of the building was engaging and informative. I gave him a brief yet impactful elevator pitch about myself, capitalizing on the short time we had.

The experience taught me a valuable lesson: every interaction is an opportunity. Whether it's an interview, a sales pitch, or a chance meeting, each moment is a chance to showcase oneself. The courage to walk into Intuit that day, coupled with my quick thinking and self-promotion skills, opened a new avenue in my career that I had never imagined.

This episode was a turning point, marking the beginning of a 10-year journey in the tech industry. This path has led me to work with giants like Amazon, QuickBooks, McAfee, Crowdstrike, and Facebook. My roles have varied from sales to engineering, each position adding a new layer to my expertise and understanding of the tech world.

My journey through the tech industry has been nothing short of an adventure, filled with learning and unexpected turns. After the fortuitous incident at Intuit, I embarked on a path that took me through the halls of some of the most influential tech companies in the world. At each stop, I embraced a new role, learning and adapting, always applying the lessons from my past experiences.

At Amazon, I delved deep into the world of e-commerce and cloud computing, understanding the intricacies of a global marketplace. My time at QuickBooks allowed me to explore financial software, aiding small businesses and individuals in managing their finances more efficiently. McAfee and Crowdstrike introduced me to the critical world of cybersecurity, where I learned about the importance of protecting digital assets in an increasingly connected world.

Perhaps one of the most impactful experiences was my time at Facebook. Here, I was exposed to the cutting edge of social media and digital communication. It was a unique opportunity to see firsthand how technology can connect people across the globe and the responsibilities that come with such power.

Throughout these experiences, I realized that my diverse background in communications, business, tech, art, and athletics was not just a list of interests, but a powerful amalgam that gave me a unique perspective in the tech world. My ability to see things from different angles, to understand the needs of various stakeholders, and to communicate effectively across different domains became my greatest strength.

As I reflect on my journey, a few key lessons stand out. First, never underestimate the power of a bold move. Walking into Intuit that day was a risk, but it paid off in ways I could never have imagined. Second, every experience, no matter how seemingly insignificant, can teach you something valuable. My time as a Lyft driver, an athlete, and a student all contributed to my success in the tech industry.

Lastly, and perhaps most importantly, is the power of self-belief and perseverance. There were moments of doubt and setbacks, but believing in my abilities and persisting through challenges has been crucial. Whether it was during my early days playing football or walking into a random building with my resume, the belief that I could make an impact made all the difference.

Today, I stand as a testament to the idea that with courage, creativity, and a willingness to seize opportunities, one can carve out a path to success, even through the most unexpected routes. My story is not just about a career in tech; it's about the journey of a Renaissance man who found his way by embracing every part of his identity and every twist and turn of his path.

This journey has been more than just a career; it's been a life lesson in adaptability, perseverance, and the power of a diverse skill set. It's a reminder that our backgrounds, experiences, and even our unexpected detours can lead us to incredible destinations.

As I stand today, reflecting on my 10-year odyssey through the tech industry, I realize that my story is one of constant evolution and learning. It's a narrative that underscores the significance of adaptability, resilience, and the willingness to embrace change. From the football fields of Detroit to the innovative corridors of Silicon Valley, my journey is a testament to the power of diversity in skills and experiences.

My path has been far from linear. It's been a mosaic of different roles, companies, and industries, each contributing to my growth. This multifaceted career has not only enriched my professional life but has also shaped my personal philosophy. I've learned that the most impactful innovations often come from the intersection of various fields and disciplines. My background in sports, arts, and business, combined with my tech expertise, has allowed me to approach problems with a unique perspective and to find creative solutions.

The lessons I've learned extend beyond the confines of the office. They have taught me about the importance of networking, the art of negotiation, and the value of a diverse professional portfolio. In every role, whether in sales, engineering, or management, I've strived to bring a holistic approach, considering not just the technical aspects but also the human element.

One of the most profound realizations has been the importance of mentorship and community. In my journey, I've had the privilege of both learning from and mentoring others. Sharing knowledge and experiences has not only helped others in their paths but has also provided me with fresh insights and perspectives.

My story is also one of resilience. The tech industry, with its rapid pace and constant evolution, can be unforgiving. There have been moments of uncertainty and failure, but each has been a stepping stone to greater understanding and success. I've learned to view challenges not as obstacles but as opportunities to grow and to innovate.

Looking ahead, I see a future where I continue to leverage my diverse experiences. I envision contributing to groundbreaking projects, mentoring the next generation of tech enthusiasts, and perhaps venturing into new, unexplored territories. The tech world is an ever-evolving landscape, and I intend to remain a dynamic participant in its journey.

In closing, my narrative is more than just a personal success story; it's a blueprint for anyone navigating the complexities of their career path. It shows that with determination, flexibility, and a willingness to step outside one's comfort zone, it's possible to carve a unique path and leave a lasting impact. As I continue my journey, I remain committed to learning, growing, and inspiring others to chase their dreams, no matter how unconventional they may seem.

Introduction: The Black Dollar's Evolution

In the epoch of rapid technological evolution and global connectivity, the concept of the Black Dollar has undergone a significant transformation, transcending beyond mere currency to symbolize a movement, a culture, and a beacon of potential for the African-American community. "A New Nation inside of a Nation – The Age of the Black Dollar" is not just a book; it is a manifesto, a guiding light for a community at the cusp of an economic renaissance. It beckons a profound shift in the thought process, particularly in the Black community, adapting the enduring legacies of icons like Martin Luther King Jr., Marcus Garvey, Malcolm X, and W.E.B. Du Bois to the digital age.

This book aims to forge a path towards a decentralized, technologically-empowered government. It's a vision where the Black Dollar circulates primarily within the Black community, bolstered by innovative investment strategies and the power of digital transformation. The concept of creating a virtual Black Wall Street is not merely a dream; it's a tangible goal, achievable through the smart application of technology and communal unity. This digital empowerment serves as a counter-narrative to the systemic barriers that have historically hindered African-American economic progress.

Moreover, the narrative delves into the complex dynamics of the African-American identity and its economic implications. It challenges the reader to reconsider the concept of reparations – not as a thing owed but as a future to be built. The idea is to establish a self-sustaining economic ecosystem that leverages the strengths of the African diaspora and the technological advancements of the modern age.

The African-American spending power, estimated to be in the billions, is a testament to the community's economic potential. This book proposes a radical redirection of this spending power back into the community through strategic investments in real estate, digital assets, and black-owned businesses. The notion of '40 acres' transcends its historical connotation to embody a future where African-Americans can claim their economic space, both literally and figuratively.

Furthermore, this work explores the role of Africa in this grand vision. It suggests that the key to unlocking the full potential of the African-American community lies in strengthening ties with the African continent. The synergy between African Americans and their ancestral homeland can be a powerhouse for economic growth and stability, facilitated by modern tools like cryptocurrency, NFTs, and peer-to-peer investing.

"A New Nation inside of a Nation – The Age of the Black Dollar" is not just about economic empowerment. It is a call to embrace our heritage, to build a future where the Black community is not only a participant in the economy but a dominant force shaping it. It's about turning the scars of the past into the blueprints for a prosperous, self-sufficient future. This book is an invitation to embark on a journey towards economic liberation and empowerment, one where the Black Dollar is not just spent but invested wisely to build a legacy for generations to come.

In this transformative era, the fusion of time-honored Black ideologies with contemporary technology offers a groundbreaking perspective on economic empowerment and social justice. "A New Nation inside of a Nation - The Age of the Black Dollar" embarks on this journey, interweaving the profound philosophies of Black leaders with the innovations of the digital age. This synthesis is not just a blend of past and present but a roadmap for a future where technology is the catalyst for economic and social change within the African-American community.

The digital age brings with it tools of unprecedented power – blockchain, cryptocurrency, NFTs, and peer-to-peer networks. These technologies are more than just new ways to conduct transactions; they represent a paradigm shift in how we view ownership, wealth distribution, and community empowerment. The ideals of self-reliance, economic independence, and social justice championed by leaders like Marcus Garvey and Malcolm X find new expressions in this digital landscape. The vision of Martin Luther King Jr. for economic justice and W.E.B. Du Bois's concept of double consciousness are reimagined in a world where digital platforms provide new avenues for expression and organization.

The concept of a decentralized government using technology is particularly revolutionary. It suggests a framework where the Black community can exercise more control over their economic destiny. This new system would bypass traditional barriers and gatekeepers, offering direct access to markets and capital. It's an embodiment of Garvey's vision of self-reliance, but on a global and digital scale.

Moreover, the idea of a virtual Black Wall Street is a direct response to the historical destruction of Black wealth and business. It symbolizes not just a recovery of what was lost, but an evolution into something more resilient and powerful. By leveraging digital technologies, African-Americans can create an economic stronghold that is immune to the physical and systemic attacks that have plagued them in the past.

Digital currencies and assets open up possibilities for wealth creation that are independent of the traditional financial systems, which have often been discriminatory. Cryptocurrencies and NFTs, when utilized effectively, can provide African-Americans with a new form of investment and asset ownership, free from the constraints of traditional banking systems. This aligns perfectly with Malcolm X's advocacy for economic empowerment as a path to freedom.

Furthermore, the use of technology to create exclusive digital realms for art, music, and real estate aligns with the pursuit of economic self-sufficiency and the celebration of Black culture. Smart contracts in blockchain technology can be used to ensure that Black creators retain control and receive fair compensation for their work, embodying Du Bois's ideology of double consciousness by providing a platform for African-American voices to be heard and valued on their own terms.

The fusion of Black ideologies with contemporary technology as presented in this book is not just about adapting to the new digital age. It's about harnessing these powerful tools to redefine the economic landscape, to build a future where the Black community can thrive economically and culturally. It's a call to action for African-Americans to become architects of their destiny, using technology as the cornerstone of a new and prosperous era.

Chapter 1: Foundations: Pillars of Black Thought

Martin's Dream: Beyond Nonviolence to Economic Justice

In exploring the foundational pillars of Black thought, we turn our attention to one of the most influential figures in American history, Dr. Martin Luther King Jr. Renowned for his leadership in the Civil Rights Movement and his unwavering commitment to nonviolence, King's philosophy extended far beyond these realms, deeply into the territory of economic justice. In "A New Nation inside of a Nation – The Age of the Black Dollar," we delve into this often lesser-discussed aspect of King's dream, viewing it through the lens of modern economic empowerment for the African-American community.

King's articulation of economic justice was rooted in a vision where all individuals, irrespective of their race, had equal opportunities to prosper. He believed that civil rights were inextricably linked to economic rights. His fight for equality was not just about the ability to sit at a lunch counter alongside whites but also about having the financial means to afford the meal. This perspective is crucial for understanding the evolution of the Black Dollar and its role in creating a self-sustaining economic ecosystem within the Black community.

In his later years, King focused increasingly on poverty and the structural economic inequalities that affected Black Americans. He advocated for a radical redistribution of economic power, a vision that aligns seamlessly with the concept of a digital Black Wall Street. King's Poor People's Campaign, for instance, was a testament to his belief in economic solidarity among the disenfranchised, transcending racial lines for a common economic agenda. His vision was for a society where wealth was not concentrated in the hands of a few but was evenly distributed to provide dignity and opportunity for all.

The "New Nation" concept takes inspiration from King's economic teachings, advocating for a world where technology is leveraged to democratize wealth and opportunity. In the digital age, economic barriers that once seemed insurmountable can now be overcome. Cryptocurrencies, digital investments, and online marketplaces present new avenues for wealth creation and distribution, reflecting King's aspirations for economic equality and justice.

Moreover, King's dream resonates with the need for financial literacy and empowerment within the Black community. His call for a guaranteed income and the creation of jobs speaks to a broader vision of economic inclusivity and empowerment.

This book builds on that vision, advocating for educational initiatives and platforms that empower African-Americans to understand and leverage financial tools to build wealth and stability.

King's dream of economic justice is not just a historical footnote but a living, breathing ideal that finds new relevance and urgency in the digital age. It's about moving beyond the fight for basic rights to securing a future of economic prosperity and stability. By embracing the principles of economic justice that King championed, the Black community can forge a path toward lasting prosperity and redefine the meaning and power of the Black Dollar.

Additional Perspectives on Martin Luther King's Ideology

Dr. Martin Luther King Jr.'s ideology, often highlighted for its advocacy of nonviolence and civil rights, encompassed a broader, more profound vision for social and economic justice. In examining this aspect further, we unveil dimensions of King's thought that resonate powerfully with contemporary efforts to empower the African-American community economically.

King's perspectives on economic justice were intrinsically tied to his understanding of dignity and equality. He saw economic disparity not merely as a matter of financial inequity but as a fundamental breach of human dignity. King believed that economic injustice was a form of violence, silent yet as damaging as physical violence. His Poor People's Campaign was not just a political movement but a moral crusade to address the evils of poverty. In the context of today's digital age, this translates to addressing the digital divide and ensuring equitable access to economic opportunities provided by technology.

King's ideology also challenged the structural barriers in American society that perpetuated racial and economic inequalities. He advocated for changes in policies and systems that disadvantaged African-Americans. This approach is particularly relevant in the digital era, where systemic barriers can manifest in new forms such as algorithmic biases or unequal access to emerging technologies like blockchain and AI.

Furthermore, King's emphasis on community action and solidarity is a vital lesson for today. He believed in the power of collective effort and grassroots movements to bring about social change. This idea is crucial in the digital age, where community-driven initiatives can harness technology to create economic opportunities. Platforms enabling peer-to-peer lending, community investment funds, or cooperative business models in the digital space are embodiments of King's vision of community strength and solidarity.

King also recognized the importance of education in achieving economic empowerment. He stressed the need for educational reform that would provide African-Americans with the skills and knowledge necessary to succeed in an increasingly competitive economy. In the modern context, this includes digital literacy and understanding new financial tools such as cryptocurrencies, which can be gateways to economic advancement and freedom.

Lastly, King's commitment to global human rights and his understanding of the interconnectedness of struggles around the world are critical in a globalized, digitally connected world. His vision extended beyond the borders of the United States, seeing the fight for civil and economic rights as part of a global struggle for human dignity. This global perspective is essential today as the African-American community looks not just inward but also builds bridges with the African continent and the broader diaspora to create a unified economic front.

Martin Luther King Jr.'s ideology, when viewed through the lens of economic justice and applied to the contemporary digital landscape, offers invaluable insights. It underscores the need for systemic change, community solidarity, educational empowerment, and a global perspective in creating a new economic paradigm for the African-American community. These principles are more than just an extension of King's dream; they are essential components of a strategy to harness the full potential of the Black Dollar in the digital age.

Garvey's Vision: Self-reliance and Independence

Marcus Garvey, a seminal figure in Black history, championed a vision characterized by self-reliance and independence for the African-American community. His ideologies, centered on the empowerment and unification of people of African descent, hold significant relevance in the context of modern economic strategies, particularly in the digital era.

Garvey's philosophy was founded on the principle of economic self-sufficiency. He believed that true freedom and empowerment for Black people could only be achieved through economic independence. This meant building and supporting Black-owned businesses, creating job opportunities within the community, and fostering a strong sense of collective economic identity. In the digital age, this translates into harnessing online platforms to promote Black entrepreneurship, utilizing e-commerce to circulate the Black dollar within the community, and creating digital spaces that support and amplify Black-owned businesses.

A critical component of Garvey's vision was the establishment of global networks. He saw the African diaspora not as a fragmented group but as a powerful, interconnected community. Today, this idea finds resonance in the global connectivity offered by digital technology. Social media, online marketplaces, and digital communication platforms have made it easier than ever for the African-American community to connect, collaborate, and build economic networks that span continents.

Garvey also advocated for the ownership of resources and means of production. In contemporary terms, this extends beyond physical assets to include digital assets like cryptocurrencies and NFTs. By engaging in the digital economy, African-Americans can take control of new forms of wealth and revenue streams, aligning with Garvey's push for economic sovereignty.

Another aspect of Garvey's ideology was his focus on education and knowledge as tools for liberation. He understood that economic independence required not just resources but also the knowledge and skills to utilize them effectively. In the current context, this underscores the importance of digital literacy and financial education as critical tools for empowering the African-American community.

Understanding and leveraging emerging technologies and financial instruments are vital for economic self-reliance in the digital age.

Furthermore, Garvey's emphasis on pride in African heritage and the rejection of colonial narratives is particularly relevant in an era where cultural representation and identity are increasingly being played out in digital realms. By promoting a narrative of strength, resilience, and pride in African-American and African heritage, there is an opportunity to reshape perceptions and build a strong, positive identity that fuels economic and social empowerment.

Marcus Garvey's vision of self-reliance and independence offers a timeless blueprint for economic empowerment. In the context of the digital age, his principles encourage the African-American community to embrace technology as a means of economic liberation, to build global networks for collective prosperity, and to foster a sense of pride and ownership over their economic future. Garvey's ideologies, thus, form a critical pillar of thought in building a new economic paradigm for the Black community in the age of digital transformation.

Exploring the Depth of Garvey's Vision

Delving deeper into Marcus Garvey's vision reveals a multifaceted approach to Black empowerment, with lessons that are remarkably applicable in today's digital and globalized context. Garvey, a proponent of the Back-to-Africa movement and the founder of the Universal Negro Improvement Association (UNIA), envisioned a future where African-Americans could achieve complete economic independence and cultural autonomy.

A key aspect of Garvey's vision was the emphasis on African pride and self-identity. He encouraged people of African descent to embrace their heritage and to build a collective identity based on shared history and aspirations. This concept transcends into the digital age as a call for African-Americans to use digital platforms to celebrate their culture, disseminate their narratives, and counteract the stereotypes often perpetuated by mainstream media. In the realm of social media, content creation, and digital storytelling, there is a powerful opportunity to shape a global understanding of Black identity in line with Garvey's teachings.

Garvey's advocacy for economic self-reliance also extended to the idea of creating and controlling Black institutions and enterprises. He believed in the power of economic autonomy as a means of resisting oppression and establishing a self-sustaining community. Today, this can be seen in the push for Black-owned businesses, Black-led tech startups, and initiatives that drive investment within the community. The digital economy offers a fertile ground for this, providing platforms for Black entrepreneurs to reach global markets and for the community to support these businesses through online patronage and crowdfunding.

Furthermore, Garvey's vision included a global dimension, recognizing the interconnectedness of African people worldwide. He saw the potential in uniting the African diaspora for mutual economic and social benefit. In the contemporary world, this global network can be realized through digital communication tools, enabling real-time collaboration and exchange of ideas, resources, and support across borders. By leveraging these connections, the African-American community can tap into a wider pool of opportunities, expertise, and markets.

Garvey also understood the importance of owning and controlling the means of production and distribution. In the modern context, this extends to digital resources and infrastructure. African-Americans engaging in digital content creation, technology development, and online commerce effectively embody this principle, taking control of their economic destiny in the digital realm.

In addition, Garvey's push for educational upliftment within the Black community remains pertinent. In an era where information is power, access to digital education and resources is crucial. Equipping the community with skills in technology, finance, and digital literacy is fundamental in actualizing Garvey's vision of self-reliance and empowerment.

Exploring the depth of Garvey's vision in the context of the digital age reveals a powerful framework for economic empowerment and cultural pride. His principles of self-identity, economic autonomy, global unity, and education provide a robust foundation for African-Americans to build upon in the pursuit of their economic and social objectives in today's interconnected world. Garvey's ideology, thus, continues to be a beacon of inspiration and guidance for the Black community as they navigate the challenges and opportunities of the digital era.

Malcolm X's Assertion: Economic Empowerment and Restitution

Malcolm X's contribution to Black thought, particularly his assertions on economic empowerment and restitution, offers a critical perspective in the context of African-American socio-economic upliftment. His ideas, marked by a distinct call for self-determination and economic independence, resonate profoundly in the pursuit of financial autonomy in the African-American community.

Central to Malcolm X's philosophy was the concept of economic self-sufficiency as a means of liberation. He challenged the African-American community to take control of their economic destiny, advocating for the creation and support of Black-owned businesses and financial institutions. This approach directly addresses the systemic barriers that have historically impeded Black economic progress, suggesting a form of empowerment that extends beyond social and political rights to encompass financial autonomy. In today's digital age, this translates into harnessing online platforms for Black entrepreneurship, embracing e-commerce, and utilizing digital tools to foster economic growth within the community.

Malcolm X also emphasized the importance of education in achieving economic empowerment. He believed that a comprehensive understanding of economics and financial literacy was essential for the African-American community to break free from the cycles of poverty and dependency. In the contemporary digital landscape, this means ensuring access to education and resources in financial literacy, digital skills, and entrepreneurship. By empowering individuals with knowledge and skills, the community can effectively navigate and leverage the digital economy for wealth creation and economic stability.

Furthermore, Malcolm's advocacy for restitution speaks to a broader narrative of economic justice. He recognized the historical injustices and systemic inequalities that have plagued African-

Americans, calling for measures to rectify these wrongs. Today, this could involve policies and initiatives that support wealth redistribution, investment in Black communities, and reparative economic measures. The digital age offers new avenues for this, such as crowdfunding platforms for community projects, blockchain technology for transparent and equitable financial transactions, and digital advocacy campaigns for policy change.

Malcolm X's assertive stance on economic empowerment also entailed a global perspective. He saw the struggles of African-Americans as part of a larger global fight against colonialism and imperialism. In the modern context, this global outlook can be materialized through digital platforms that connect the African-American community with the African diaspora, fostering international trade, collaboration, and cultural exchange.

Lastly, Malcolm X's call for unity and collective action in economic endeavors is particularly relevant in the age of social media and online communities. By building networks of support, sharing resources, and collaborating on economic ventures, the African-American community can amplify their economic impact and create a resilient economic ecosystem.

Malcolm X's perspectives on economic empowerment and restitution provide a potent framework for African-American economic strategy. His ideas about self-sufficiency, education, restitution, global solidarity, and collective action offer invaluable insights for leveraging digital technologies to achieve economic freedom and justice. His legacy continues to inspire and guide efforts towards creating a more equitable and prosperous future for the African-American community.

Further Insights into Malcolm X's Economic Views

Diving deeper into Malcolm X's economic views uncovers a rich, nuanced understanding of the challenges and potential pathways for African-American economic empowerment. His perspectives, though rooted in the mid-20th century struggles, have enduring relevance, particularly when aligned with contemporary economic strategies and digital advancements.

One of the cornerstones of Malcolm X's economic philosophy was the concept of "Black Nationalism," which advocated for the control of the economic resources within the African-American community. This meant not only creating and supporting Black-owned businesses but also ensuring that the Black community was the primary beneficiary of these economic activities. In today's context, this translates into a focused drive towards creating and nurturing a digital economic ecosystem that is by and for African-Americans. This includes e-commerce platforms that prioritize Black vendors, apps that facilitate economic transactions within the Black community, and digital marketplaces that celebrate and sell Black art, music, and literature.

Malcolm X also stressed the importance of financial independence from systems that he viewed as oppressive and exploitative. He believed that economic independence was inextricably linked to political freedom and social justice. In the digital age, this independence can be pursued through innovative financial tools such as cryptocurrency, which offers a way to participate in economic activities outside of traditional banking systems. This approach is particularly empowering in a context where African-Americans have often faced systemic financial exclusion and discrimination.

Another critical aspect of Malcolm X's economic thought was his emphasis on internationalism. He consistently highlighted the interconnectedness of the African-American struggle with that of oppressed peoples globally. This global perspective is vital today as digital technologies enable international commerce and communication. The African-American community can leverage these global networks for economic growth, tapping into markets and resources beyond the United States and fostering economic partnerships with the African continent and the broader diaspora.

Malcolm's views also included a strong component of self-education and knowledge acquisition. He was a proponent of learning as a tool for liberation, emphasizing the need for African-Americans to educate themselves about the economic systems and practices that govern their lives. In the era of information technology, this education is more accessible than ever. Online courses, webinars, and digital libraries can provide the community with knowledge on financial management, investment strategies, and the intricacies of the digital economy.

Lastly, Malcolm X's economic philosophy recognized the power of collective action. He saw strength in unity and collaboration, advocating for cooperative economics within the African-American community. This principle is particularly relevant in the context of social media and online platforms, where communities can come together to support Black businesses, crowdfund community projects, and share economic resources and opportunities.

Exploring Malcolm X's economic views in greater depth reveals a comprehensive blueprint for economic empowerment in the African-American community. His emphasis on self-reliance, financial independence, international solidarity, education, and collective action provides invaluable guidance for harnessing the opportunities of the digital age. These insights form a foundational pillar in the quest to build a prosperous and equitable economic future for African-Americans.

Du Bois's Duality: Navigating Double Consciousness

W.E.B. Du Bois's concept of double consciousness is a fundamental component in understanding the African-American experience, particularly in the context of economic empowerment and identity. His theory, which describes an internal conflict faced by subordinated groups in an oppressive society, is crucial for comprehending the challenges and opportunities in the African-American journey towards economic self-sufficiency.

Du Bois described double consciousness as a sense of always looking at oneself through the eyes of others, of measuring one's soul by the tape of a world that looks on in amused contempt and pity. For African-Americans, this meant constantly negotiating between their African heritage and the American culture in which they lived. This duality can be seen in the economic sphere, where African-Americans often navigate between mainstream economic practices and those that resonate more deeply with their cultural and communal identity.

In the digital age, this duality presents both challenges and opportunities. On one hand, African-Americans have the potential to harness technology to create and participate in economic systems that reflect their values and cultural heritage. Digital platforms can be used to promote Black-owned businesses, support community-based projects, and create spaces where African-American consumers and entrepreneurs can interact in ways that are culturally affirming and economically beneficial.

On the other hand, the digital world also replicates some of the systemic biases and barriers that exist in the physical world. African-Americans engaging in online commerce or digital finance may still face issues related to discrimination or lack of access to capital. Navigating this digital landscape requires an acute awareness of the dual realities that Du Bois articulated, balancing the need to operate within mainstream systems while also working to create and support alternative, community-centered economic structures.

Furthermore, Du Bois's concept of double consciousness also speaks to the psychological and cultural aspects of economic empowerment. It involves a conscious effort to embrace and affirm African-American identity and heritage in the face of economic systems that have historically undervalued or exploited Black communities. This means not only seeking economic success but also redefining what success looks like in a way that is authentic and empowering for the African-American community.

In addition, Du Bois's ideas about the "Talented Tenth" – a leadership class that would rise to uplift the entire African-American community – can be applied in the context of digital leadership and innovation. African-Americans who excel in fields like technology, finance, and digital entrepreneurship have a crucial role to play in leading and inspiring the broader community towards economic empowerment.

Navigating Du Bois's concept of double consciousness in the modern economic landscape involves a multifaceted approach. It requires an acknowledgment of the unique challenges faced by African-Americans, an embrace of cultural identity in economic endeavors, and a concerted effort to build and support economic systems that are equitable, inclusive, and reflective of African-American values and experiences. Understanding and addressing this duality is essential for achieving true economic empowerment and self-sufficiency for the African-American community.

Expanding on Du Bois's Concept of Double Consciousness

Expanding on W.E.B. Du Bois's concept of double consciousness involves exploring its implications in the modern era, especially in the context of economic empowerment and digital innovation. Double consciousness, as Du Bois described, is the sensation of looking at oneself through the lens of a racially prejudiced society and the struggle to reconcile an African heritage with a European upbringing and education. In the 21st century, this concept takes on new dimensions as African-Americans navigate the complexities of identity in a digital and globally connected world.

Firstly, the idea of double consciousness can be extended to the realm of digital identity. African-Americans today are often required to navigate between their real-life identities and how they present themselves in digital spaces. The internet, social media, and digital platforms offer both an opportunity to express a more authentic self but can also be spaces where racial prejudices are perpetuated. Balancing these spaces requires a nuanced understanding of how digital personas can both liberate and confine African-American identities.

Moreover, in terms of economic empowerment, double consciousness manifests in the choices African-Americans make in their economic activities. It involves the reconciliation of participating in a predominantly white, capitalist economy while also striving to build and support a parallel economy that is rooted in Black culture and community. This duality is evident in the way African-American consumers and entrepreneurs must navigate a market system that often marginalizes or exploits them, while also creating spaces and opportunities that uplift Black economic interests.

The concept also has significant implications for leadership within the African-American community. Du Bois's notion of the "Talented Tenth" suggested that a small, educated elite would lead the way for the race. In the context of double consciousness, this raises questions about who leads, who follows, and how leadership is cultivated and maintained in a community that is constantly balancing between two worlds. It also calls for a reevaluation of what constitutes leadership and success in a society where racial dynamics are ever-present.

Furthermore, double consciousness affects the way African-Americans engage with technology and innovation. While digital technologies offer new avenues for economic growth and expression, they can also replicate existing inequalities. African-Americans in the tech industry must navigate these dual realities, contributing to a sector that has historically been dominated by white males, while also ensuring that the benefits of technological innovation reach the Black community.

Lastly, expanding on double consciousness means recognizing its global aspect. In an interconnected world, the experiences of African-Americans are linked to those of Black people globally. This global double consciousness involves negotiating the realities of being both a member of the global African diaspora and a citizen of a specific nation with its own unique racial dynamics.

Du Bois's concept of double consciousness, when expanded, offers a rich framework for understanding the complexities of African-American identity in the modern world. It encapsulates the ongoing struggle to navigate and reconcile the multiple facets of being Black in America, particularly in the realms of economic empowerment and digital engagement. Understanding and addressing these dynamics is crucial for the development of strategies that foster true economic and cultural empowerment for the African-American community.

Chapter 2: Modern Paradigms: The Digital Dawn

Digital Age and Black Empowerment

The advent of the digital age has ushered in unprecedented opportunities for empowerment, particularly for historically marginalized communities like African-Americans. This era, characterized by rapid technological advancements and global connectivity, offers a new paradigm for Black empowerment, redefining traditional barriers and creating innovative pathways to economic and social prosperity.

At the heart of this digital empowerment is the democratization of access to information and resources. The internet has become a critical tool for education, providing access to a wealth of knowledge that was previously unavailable or inaccessible to many in the African-American community. From online courses and tutorials to vast repositories of cultural and historical information, the digital world offers an expansive platform for learning and personal development. This access to knowledge is a powerful equalizer, enabling African-Americans to gain the skills and information needed to compete in an increasingly digital economy.

Moreover, the digital age has transformed the landscape of entrepreneurship and business. E-commerce and digital marketplaces have lowered the barriers to entry for African-American entrepreneurs, allowing them to bypass traditional gatekeepers and reach a global audience. Social media platforms have become powerful tools for marketing and brand building, enabling Black businesses to connect with customers and communities in ways that were previously unimaginable. This shift has not only spurred economic growth within the Black community but has also fostered a greater sense of agency and self-reliance.

Another significant aspect of digital empowerment is the emergence of new forms of financial technology. Cryptocurrencies, blockchain technology, and mobile banking have opened up alternative avenues for financial transactions and investments. For African-Americans, who have often faced systemic barriers in traditional banking systems, these digital financial tools offer a path to financial inclusion and empowerment. They provide a means of participating in the economy on more equitable terms, enabling wealth creation and financial autonomy.

The digital age also facilitates community building and collective action. Online platforms and social networks have become vital spaces for African-Americans to connect, share experiences, and mobilize around social and economic issues. From crowdfunding community projects to organizing social justice movements, the digital world provides a powerful medium for collective voice and action. This has not only strengthened community bonds but has also amplified the influence and impact of the African-American community.

Furthermore, the digital landscape offers a unique opportunity for cultural expression and representation. African-American artists, creators, and storytellers are using digital media to convey their narratives, challenge stereotypes, and showcase the richness of Black culture. This creative expression is not just an artistic endeavor; it's a form of empowerment, reshaping perceptions and reinforcing a strong and positive Black identity.

The digital age presents a new dawn for Black empowerment, marked by increased access to knowledge, entrepreneurial opportunities, financial tools, community solidarity, and cultural expression. As the African-American community navigates this digital landscape, it holds the potential to transform traditional power dynamics, foster economic and social prosperity, and redefine what it means to be empowered in the 21st century.

Modern Paradigms: The Digital Dawn

Continuing the exploration of digital empowerment in the African-American context, we delve deeper into how the digital revolution is reshaping the landscape of opportunity, community, and identity. The digital dawn, while presenting new avenues for growth and expression, also brings with it challenges and responsibilities that must be navigated with insight and foresight.

One of the pivotal aspects of digital empowerment is the role of technology in reshaping economic structures. The rise of the gig economy, digital entrepreneurship, and e-commerce has created new job opportunities and income streams. For the African-American community, this shift offers a chance to bypass traditional barriers in the job market and achieve financial independence. However, it also requires adaptability and a new set of digital skills. Therefore, investment in digital literacy and technology education becomes crucial, ensuring that the community is not left behind in the rapidly evolving digital job market.

The digital realm also offers an unprecedented platform for networking and collaboration. Social media, online forums, and digital conferences enable African-Americans to connect with peers, mentors, and industry leaders worldwide. These connections can lead to collaborative projects, mentorship opportunities, and the sharing of resources and knowledge that are vital for personal and professional growth. However, navigating these networks requires a critical understanding of digital identity and privacy, as well as the ability to discern and engage with constructive and beneficial online communities.

Furthermore, the digital age has revolutionized access to financial services and investment opportunities. Digital banking, cryptocurrencies, and online investment platforms offer more inclusive access to financial resources. These tools can be particularly empowering for communities that have traditionally faced barriers in accessing financial services. They also present new avenues for community-based economic initiatives, such as crowdfunding for local projects or investment clubs focused on supporting Black-owned businesses. Yet, these opportunities also necessitate a comprehensive understanding of digital finance, risk assessment, and responsible investment practices.

Another critical dimension of digital empowerment is the potential for advocacy and social change. Digital platforms have become powerful tools for raising awareness about social justice issues, mobilizing community action, and holding institutions accountable. The African-American community has leveraged these platforms to amplify their voice and impact in areas like civil rights, education, and political engagement. However, this also involves challenges related to misinformation, online harassment, and the need for sustainable digital activism strategies.

Lastly, the digital age provides a canvas for cultural expression and identity formation. Through digital art, online storytelling, and content creation, African-Americans can express their heritage, experiences, and aspirations. This digital cultural expression is not just an act of creativity; it's a form of empowerment, contributing to a diverse and rich online landscape. However, it also requires vigilance against digital appropriation and the commodification of cultural elements, ensuring that digital spaces respect and honor the authenticity of Black culture.

The continued discussion on digital empowerment underscores the multifaceted impact of the digital age on the African-American community. It highlights the potential for economic growth, community building, financial inclusion, social advocacy, and cultural expression, balanced with the need for education, critical engagement, and an awareness of the challenges inherent in the digital world. As we embrace the opportunities of the digital dawn, a thoughtful and strategic approach is essential to harness its full potential for empowerment and transformation.

Legacy of the Panthers: Unity in Modern Context

The Black Panther Party, established in the 1960s, left an indelible mark on the struggle for African-American rights. Their legacy, particularly in fostering unity and community empowerment, finds renewed relevance in the modern context, especially in the era of digital connectivity. Understanding and adapting the Panthers' principles to the current digital age offers insightful pathways for promoting unity and collective strength within the African-American community.

Central to the Black Panthers' philosophy was the concept of self-determination and community service. They established programs like free breakfast for children and community health clinics, demonstrating the power of grassroots initiatives in addressing community needs. In today's digital world, this spirit of community service can be revitalized through online platforms. Social media, crowdfunding, and digital organizing tools enable the African-American community to mobilize resources, provide support, and address social issues effectively and efficiently. Digital platforms can facilitate the creation of modern equivalents to the Panthers' community programs, offering a wide range of services from educational resources to health and financial literacy.

Another significant aspect of the Panthers' legacy is their emphasis on education and knowledge as tools for empowerment. They understood that true liberation required an informed and conscious community. In the digital era, this translates into access to online educational resources, digital literacy programs, and platforms that provide information on civil rights, legal aid, and social services. Digital media also offers a means to counteract mainstream narratives, allowing the African-American community to tell their own stories and disseminate information that is relevant and empowering to their experiences and struggles.

The Panthers were also notable for their efforts in building alliances across different communities and groups. They understood the power of solidarity in combating systemic oppression. In the digital age, this approach is more feasible and impactful than ever. The internet allows for the formation of global networks of solidarity, connecting the African-American struggle with other movements around the world. Through digital platforms, there can be a unified voice against injustice, sharing strategies, and support across borders, and fostering a sense of global community among oppressed groups.

Moreover, the Black Panthers' focus on self-defense and community policing has contemporary implications in the context of ongoing concerns about law enforcement and racial profiling. Digital technology offers tools for community monitoring, legal awareness, and advocacy. Mobile applications, online forums, and social media can be used to document incidents, share legal advice, and mobilize community responses to instances of injustice.

Finally, the Panthers' emphasis on self-respect and Black pride can be mirrored in the digital age through the promotion of positive Black identities online. Digital platforms offer spaces to celebrate Black culture, achievements, and history, contributing to a sense of pride and unity within the community.

The legacy of the Black Panther Party provides enduring lessons and strategies that can be adapted to the modern digital context. Their principles of community service, education, alliance-building, self-defense, and pride in Black identity offer a powerful blueprint for fostering unity and empowerment within the African-American community in today's interconnected world.

The Ongoing Influence of the Black Panthers

The Black Panther Party's influence extends far beyond its historical context, permeating into the fabric of modern African-American struggles and triumphs. Their groundbreaking approach to civil rights, community empowerment, and social justice continues to resonate, particularly in the context of today's digital age. Understanding and embracing the ongoing influence of the Black Panthers can provide valuable insights for contemporary movements and initiatives within the African-American community.

One of the most enduring aspects of the Black Panthers' legacy is their focus on community-based solutions to systemic problems. They recognized that real change often starts at the local level, through programs and initiatives directly addressing community needs. In the digital age, this philosophy is more applicable than ever. Online platforms and digital tools enable communities to organize, fundraise, and implement solutions tailored to their specific contexts. From virtual town halls discussing community issues to crowdfunding campaigns for local projects, the Panthers' approach to community activism has found new life in the digital world.

The Black Panthers were also pioneers in using media to counteract negative stereotypes and disseminate their message. Their use of newsletters and community newspapers played a crucial role in educating and mobilizing support. Today, social media and digital content platforms serve a similar purpose, offering African-American communities a space to control their narrative, challenge mainstream media biases, and foster a sense of solidarity and shared purpose. The digital dissemination of news, stories, and perspectives continues the Panthers' tradition of independent, community-focused media.

Another key aspect of the Black Panthers' influence is their emphasis on the importance of education and knowledge. They set up free breakfast programs and community schools, recognizing that empowerment starts with access to knowledge and resources. In the modern digital landscape, similar principles can be applied through online education platforms, e-learning resources, and virtual mentorship programs. Providing the community with digital tools and knowledge not only equips them to succeed in the modern world but also upholds the Panthers' belief in education as a cornerstone of empowerment.

Moreover, the Panthers' dedication to fighting systemic injustice has inspired current movements advocating for racial equality and social justice. Modern activists continue to draw upon the Panthers' strategies of organizing, mobilizing, and demanding accountability. The digital age has amplified these efforts, enabling movements to gain momentum quickly, coordinate actions globally, and bring attention to issues at unprecedented scales.

Finally, the Black Panthers' commitment to Black pride and cultural affirmation remains a vital component of their ongoing influence. They celebrated Black identity and heritage, encouraging the community to take pride in their history and culture. In today's digital era, this translates into a vibrant online celebration of Black art, music, literature, and cultural heritage. Digital platforms have become spaces where the African-American community can explore and express their identity, fostering a sense of pride and belonging.

The ongoing influence of the Black Panthers in the digital age is profound and multifaceted. Their principles of community activism, media savvy, educational empowerment, social justice advocacy, and cultural affirmation continue to guide and inspire modern African-American movements and initiatives. By embracing and adapting these principles, the African-American community can leverage digital tools and platforms to continue the Panthers' legacy of empowerment and change.

Unraveling Desegregation: A Double-edged Sword

The era of desegregation, marked by the dismantling of legal segregation in the United States, was a significant turning point in American history. However, its impact on the African-American community has been a double-edged sword, bringing both progress and new challenges, especially in the context of the digital age.

Desegregation was a monumental victory in the fight for civil rights, symbolizing a legal and moral recognition of equality. It opened doors to educational and employment opportunities that were previously denied to African-Americans. However, the process of integrating into previously all-white spaces also led to the dilution of Black economic and social networks. The closure of Black-owned businesses and schools, once thriving centers of Black community life, resulted in a loss of economic autonomy and cultural solidarity.

In the digital era, the legacy of desegregation has taken on new dimensions. On one hand, digital platforms have broken down barriers, offering African-Americans access to a wider range of economic and educational opportunities. The internet serves as a great equalizer, providing resources and platforms where race is ostensibly less of a barrier than in physical spaces. African-Americans can leverage these digital spaces for entrepreneurship, education, and networking, transcending geographical and social limitations.

On the other hand, the digital world has also mirrored and amplified some of the systemic inequalities that desegregation failed to eliminate. Issues such as digital redlining, where communities are denied equitable access to fast internet services, and algorithmic biases in hiring and lending practices, reflect ongoing racial disparities. Additionally, the ease of connectivity has sometimes inadvertently led to the further dispersal of the Black community, posing challenges to the kind of tight-knit communal bonds that characterized pre-desegregation Black life.

Moreover, desegregation has had complex implications for identity formation among African-Americans. The process of integrating into broader society has often required navigating a delicate balance between assimilation and maintaining a distinct cultural identity. In the digital realm, this is reflected in how African-Americans present themselves online, often negotiating between mainstream expectations and authentic self-expression. Social media and digital content creation offer platforms for exploring and affirming Black identity, but they can also be spaces where the pressures to conform to wider societal norms are felt.

Furthermore, desegregation has led to a reevaluation of the strategies needed to achieve racial equality. While legal segregation has ended, economic and social disparities persist. The digital age offers new tools for advocacy and activism, enabling African-Americans to mobilize effectively against ongoing injustices. Online platforms have become crucial for raising awareness, organizing communities, and holding institutions accountable.

Understanding desegregation as a double-edged sword is crucial in the digital age. While it has undoubtedly opened new avenues for progress, it has also presented unique challenges that require careful navigation. The African-American community can harness the power of digital tools to rebuild and strengthen economic and social networks, advocate for justice, and redefine identity in a post-desegregation world, continuing the journey towards true equality and empowerment.

Further Analysis of Desegregation's Impact

The impact of desegregation on the African-American community requires deeper examination, particularly when considering the long-term social and economic implications. Desegregation, a landmark achievement in the struggle for civil rights, significantly altered the landscape of American society. However, its repercussions have been complex, with both positive advancements and unintended consequences, especially when viewed through the lens of the digital era.

Desegregation brought about the integration of African-Americans into broader society, providing access to public spaces, education, and employment opportunities that were previously segregated. This integration was pivotal in breaking down the barriers of institutional racism and promoting a more inclusive society. However, this process also led to the disintegration of many Black-owned businesses and institutions that had been the backbone of African-American communities during segregation. These establishments were not only economic centers but also places of cultural and social significance. Their decline meant the loss of vital community support systems and a shift in the economic landscape for many African-Americans.

In the digital age, the impact of desegregation is seen in the way African-Americans navigate online spaces. The internet offers a platform where racial identity can be more fluid, allowing for broader engagement with diverse groups and ideas. However, this can also lead to a dilution of the strong community ties that were characteristic of the segregated era. While digital platforms provide opportunities for networking and community building, they can't fully replicate the physical spaces that fostered a strong sense of community and cultural identity.

Furthermore, desegregation's impact on education has been significant. Access to integrated schools meant exposure to broader educational resources and perspectives. Yet, this integration often came at the cost of losing culturally relevant education and mentorship, which historically Black schools provided. In the digital world, this translates into the challenge of ensuring that educational content is both inclusive and representative of African-American history and culture.

Economically, desegregation opened up new job markets and career opportunities for African-Americans. However, it also meant competing in a broader economy that often remained subtly discriminatory. The digital economy, while offering new avenues for entrepreneurship and employment, also reflects these challenges. African-Americans in the tech industry, for instance, face underrepresentation and discrimination, mirroring the broader economic disparities that desegregation was meant to address.

Moreover, desegregation has impacted social dynamics within the African-American community. The move towards integration sometimes created a divide between those who benefited from new opportunities and those who were left behind. In the digital realm, this is reflected in the digital divide, where access to technology and the internet is not uniformly available to all, exacerbating existing inequalities.

A further analysis of desegregation's impact reveals a nuanced picture. While it marked a significant step towards racial equality, it also brought challenges that continue to affect the African-American community in the digital era. Understanding these complexities is crucial for developing strategies that leverage digital tools for economic, educational, and social empowerment, while also addressing the ongoing challenges and disparities that desegregation left in its wake.

Chapter 3: Pioneering the Future: Tech and Community

Re-envisioning the Black Wall Street

The concept of the Black Wall Street, historically embodied by the prosperous African-American community of Greenwood in Tulsa, Oklahoma, stands as a symbol of Black economic self-sufficiency and success. In today's digital era, re-envisioning the Black Wall Street involves adapting its spirit to the modern economic landscape, leveraging technology to create new avenues for prosperity and community resilience.

The original Black Wall Street was a testament to what African-Americans could achieve despite systemic barriers: a thriving hub of businesses, services, and a strong sense of community. Translating this into the 21st century, the new digital Black Wall Street signifies a network of interconnected Black-owned businesses, online platforms, and tech-driven initiatives that collectively build economic strength and autonomy. This digital transformation allows for greater scalability, reach, and adaptability, transcending geographical limitations and traditional market barriers.

Central to re-envisioning the Black Wall Street in the digital age is the emphasis on technology as a tool for economic empowerment. E-commerce platforms, digital marketplaces, and fintech solutions offer unparalleled opportunities for Black entrepreneurs to launch and scale their businesses. These digital tools can democratize access to markets, provide new funding avenues, and create innovative business models tailored to the needs of the African-American community.

Furthermore, the digital Black Wall Street concept encapsulates more than just economic transactions; it represents a shift towards building a sustainable ecosystem that supports the entire lifecycle of Black-owned businesses. This includes digital incubators and accelerators focused on African-American startups, mentorship programs connecting seasoned entrepreneurs with emerging talent, and online communities where business knowledge and experiences are shared.

In addition, leveraging blockchain technology and cryptocurrencies can play a significant role in this new economic landscape. Blockchain's decentralized nature offers transparency and security, vital for building trust within the community. Cryptocurrencies and tokenization can provide new ways to fundraise, invest, and build wealth, bypassing traditional financial systems that often exclude or disadvantage African-Americans.

Education and digital literacy are also integral to re-envisioning the Black Wall Street. Providing the community with the skills and knowledge to navigate and succeed in the digital economy is essential. This involves not only technical and business education but also financial literacy and an understanding of digital rights and privacy.

The reimagined Black Wall Street also acknowledges the importance of community and cultural identity. Digital platforms can foster a sense of community, providing spaces where African-American culture and values are celebrated and where community members can support and uplift each other. This sense of belonging and mutual support is critical for replicating the communal strength that was a hallmark of the original Black Wall Street.

Re-envisioning the Black Wall Street in the digital era is about creating a comprehensive, technology-driven economic ecosystem that empowers the African-American community. It combines entrepreneurship, technology, education, and community building to create a new model of economic success and resilience, rooted in the rich legacy of the past but fully oriented towards the future.

The New Age of Black Economic Empowerment

In the new age of technology, the landscape of Black economic empowerment is undergoing a significant transformation. This era is marked by a shift from traditional methods of economic advancement to innovative approaches powered by digital technology. The potential for African-Americans to leverage these technologies to create wealth, foster community growth, and achieve financial independence has never been greater.

Firstly, the rise of digital entrepreneurship presents a groundbreaking opportunity for Black economic empowerment. With the advent of e-commerce platforms, social media marketing, and online business tools, African-Americans can start and grow businesses with reduced overhead costs and access to global markets. This democratization of entrepreneurship breaks down traditional barriers, allowing for greater participation and success in the business world. Furthermore, technology enables niche markets and community-focused businesses to thrive, catering to the specific needs and interests of the African-American community.

Another significant aspect of this new era is the emergence of fintech and alternative financial services. Traditional banking systems have often underserved African-American communities.

However, digital financial technologies like mobile banking, peer-to-peer lending platforms, and cryptocurrencies offer new ways to access capital, manage finances, and invest. These tools provide a pathway to financial inclusion, allowing individuals and communities to bypass systemic financial barriers and build wealth independently.

The digital age also redefines the concept of networking and community building. Online platforms and social networks have become essential for professional growth, mentorship, and collaboration. African-Americans can connect with peers, mentors, and industry leaders worldwide, creating a support system that fosters economic growth and empowerment. Virtual communities can also mobilize resources and support for Black-owned businesses, creating a robust ecosystem of mutual support and economic solidarity.

Moreover, the new age of Black economic empowerment is characterized by an increased focus on education and skill development. Digital literacy, technological proficiency, and entrepreneurial skills are more crucial than ever. Online courses, webinars, and digital resources provide accessible education opportunities, enabling individuals to acquire the skills needed to succeed in the modern economy. This focus on education also includes financial literacy, equipping the community to make informed decisions about investments, savings, and financial management.

Lastly, the digital era offers a platform for advocacy and social change. Digital activism can drive economic empowerment by addressing systemic issues that hinder African-American prosperity. Online campaigns, digital storytelling, and social media movements can raise awareness, influence policy, and foster a collective response to economic injustices.

The new age of Black economic empowerment in the digital era is marked by innovative approaches to entrepreneurship, finance, community building, education, and advocacy. By embracing and leveraging digital technologies, African-Americans can overcome historical barriers, create new opportunities for wealth creation, and build a sustainable future of economic prosperity and independence. This era is not just about adapting to technological changes; it's about harnessing them to redefine and achieve economic empowerment on their terms.

There is also a lot of potential for strategic empowerment and economic enhancement of black communities through targeted investment and the development of self-sustaining economic systems. Creating an ecosystem that effectively circulates the black dollar within these communities, fostering economic growth, and self-reliance. The idea is to utilize technology as a tool for empowerment – connecting businesses to consumers within these communities and beyond. This approach aims to close the wealth gap and address systemic economic disparities by promoting entrepreneurship, financial literacy, and access to capital within black communities. The ultimate goal is to create a robust economic network that supports and amplifies the wealth and resources of black people, ensuring that these communities are not just participants in the economy, but drivers of economic innovation and growth.

"40'aces": Digitally Reuniting a Community

The "40'aces" initiative represents a groundbreaking digital movement aimed at reconnecting and empowering the African-American community. Named to evoke the historical promise of "forty acres and a mule," this modern platform transcends its symbolic roots to become a tangible tool for economic and social unity. At its core, "40'aces" leverages digital technology to create a virtual space that bridges geographical divides, fosters economic collaboration, and strengthens communal bonds.

The primary objective of "40'aces" is to create a digital hub where African-Americans can engage in economic activities that directly benefit their community. This includes a marketplace for Black-owned businesses, investment opportunities in African-American ventures, and platforms for crowdfunding community projects. By centralizing these activities in a digital space, "40'aces" not only provides a boost to Black entrepreneurship but also ensures that the circulation of the Black dollar remains within the community, strengthening economic foundations.

Moreover, "40'aces" serves as a platform for financial education and resources. It offers workshops, webinars, and learning materials focused on financial literacy, investment strategies, and economic planning. These educational resources are crucial for empowering individuals with the knowledge and skills needed to navigate the financial landscape, make informed decisions, and achieve financial independence.

Another key feature of "40'aces" is its ability to foster a sense of community and collective identity. The platform provides spaces for networking, mentorship, and community discussions, allowing users to connect, share experiences, and support one another. This digital reunion of the community goes beyond mere social interaction; it facilitates a shared vision and collaborative efforts towards common goals, echoing the unity and self-reliance that characterized historical Black Wall Street communities.

"40'aces" also integrates elements of technology such as blockchain and smart contracts to ensure transparency and security in transactions. This adoption of cutting-edge technology not only modernizes economic activities but also builds trust and credibility within the platform. Users can engage in transactions, investments, and collaborations knowing that their contributions are secure and their interests are protected.

Furthermore, the platform plays a significant role in cultural preservation and promotion. "40'aces" offers a space for African-American artists, musicians, writers, and creators to showcase their work, tell their stories, and celebrate their heritage. This cultural aspect is vital for maintaining a strong and cohesive community identity, reminding users of the rich legacy and resilience of the African-American experience.

In conclusion, "40'aces" is more than just a digital platform; it is a movement towards economic self-determination and community solidarity. By harnessing the power of digital technology, it seeks to reunite the African-American community in a shared space of economic empowerment, education, and cultural celebration. "40'aces" stands as a beacon of innovation and unity, guiding the community towards a future where economic prosperity and social cohesion are achieved through the power of digital connection and collaboration.

Exploring the Potential of "40'aces"

"40'aces" represents not just a digital platform, but a dynamic movement poised to revolutionize the economic landscape for the African-American community. Its potential lies in its multifaceted approach, combining technology, education, and community empowerment to create a sustainable ecosystem of growth and prosperity. Exploring the possibilities of "40'aces" reveals how it could be a catalyst for long-lasting, positive change.

One of the most significant potentials of "40'aces" is in fostering economic self-sufficiency within the African-American community. By providing a centralized online marketplace for Black-owned businesses, the platform can significantly boost visibility and sales for these enterprises. This economic model encourages the circulation of wealth within the community, ensuring that the benefits of financial transactions contribute to the collective prosperity. Moreover, the platform can facilitate connections between Black entrepreneurs and investors, creating a nurturing environment for start-ups and innovative ventures.

In terms of financial education and empowerment, "40'aces" stands to make a substantial impact. Financial literacy is key to economic advancement, yet it remains a gap in many communities. "40'aces" can bridge this gap by offering accessible, relevant financial education tailored to the needs of its users. Through webinars, interactive courses, and resource libraries, the platform can equip individuals with knowledge in areas such as budgeting, investing, and navigating the digital economy, enabling them to make informed financial decisions and grow their wealth.

Another area where "40'aces" shows immense potential is in harnessing technology for community development. By utilizing blockchain for secure transactions and smart contracts for business deals, the platform can build a foundation of trust and efficiency. Additionally, the integration of technologies like AI for personalized recommendations and data analytics for market insights can enhance the user experience and drive strategic growth.

The platform also presents an opportunity to strengthen community bonds and foster a shared sense of identity. Through forums, discussion boards, and social networking features, "40'aces" can become a digital gathering place for African-Americans to connect, share experiences, and offer support. This sense of community is vital for collective empowerment and resilience, providing a network of support that extends beyond mere business transactions.

Furthermore, "40'aces" has the potential to be a powerful tool for advocacy and social change. By aggregating a large user base, the platform can mobilize collective action on critical issues affecting the African-American community. Whether it's campaigning for policy changes, supporting social justice initiatives, or organizing community-driven projects, "40'aces" can amplify the voice and impact of its users.

The potential of "40'aces" lies in its ability to blend technology, economic empowerment, and community solidarity in a transformative way. It's more than a platform; it's a vision for the future where the African-American community harnesses the power of digital innovation to create a self-sustaining ecosystem of prosperity and growth. "40'aces" stands as a testament to what can be achieved when technology is aligned with the values, needs, and aspirations of a community.

The initiative is conceptualized as a comprehensive empowerment program that aims to provide a wide range of resources and support to African Americans. The initiative's name evokes historical promises made to former slaves in the United States, representing a modern commitment to economic and social justice. This program is designed to be an all-encompassing ecosystem, offering tools and opportunities for building businesses, marketing, sales, investor engagement, real estate development, and education on various subjects crucial for advancement. It envisages a virtual ecosystem that leverages digital currency, providing exclusive rights to music and other cultural products, thereby ensuring that benefits flow back to the creators and their supporters. By connecting these elements to African resources and opportunities, the initiative seeks to create a powerful synergy between African Americans and their ancestral homeland, fostering economic, cultural, and technological exchanges that benefit both communities.

The Crypto Revolution: More than Digital Gold

The cryptocurrency revolution represents a seismic shift in the financial landscape, offering more than just an alternative form of digital gold. For the African-American community, it heralds a new era of economic empowerment and opportunity, challenging traditional financial systems and offering innovative pathways to wealth creation and distribution.

At its core, cryptocurrency is a decentralized digital currency, free from the control of traditional banking institutions. This decentralization is particularly significant for African-Americans, who have historically faced systemic barriers in accessing banking services and capital. Cryptocurrencies offer an alternative financial system where participation is based on technological access rather than socio-economic status or racial identity. This democratization of financial services aligns with the community's long-standing pursuit of economic justice and equality.

Beyond its basic functionality as a currency, the technology underpinning cryptocurrencies, blockchain, has profound implications for economic empowerment. Blockchain's key features – transparency, security, and immutability – make it an ideal platform for creating trust in transactions. For African-American businesses and consumers, this means the ability to engage in financial activities with a new level of confidence and security, free from the fear of bias or unequal treatment.

The investment potential of cryptocurrencies also presents a unique opportunity for wealth generation within the African-American community. While traditional investment avenues often have high barriers to entry, cryptocurrencies are more accessible, allowing individuals to start with relatively small investments. This accessibility, combined with the potential for high returns, makes cryptocurrencies an attractive option for community members looking to grow their wealth.

Furthermore, cryptocurrencies enable innovative models of fundraising and community support. Through initial coin offerings (ICOs) and tokenization, African-American entrepreneurs have new avenues for raising capital for their ventures. Community projects can similarly benefit from these models, tapping into a broader base of support beyond traditional funding sources. This approach not only provides necessary funds but also fosters a sense of communal ownership and investment in the success of community-driven initiatives.

Another key aspect of the crypto revolution is its potential to facilitate remittances and international transactions. For African-Americans with familial or business ties abroad, particularly in Africa and the Caribbean, cryptocurrencies offer a cost-effective and efficient means of sending money across borders. This can strengthen international connections and contribute to a global network of economic collaboration and support.

However, the crypto revolution also comes with its challenges, including market volatility, regulatory uncertainties, and the need for digital literacy. Navigating these challenges requires education and caution, ensuring that community members are well-informed about the risks and opportunities associated with cryptocurrencies.

The cryptocurrency revolution is more than just a new form of digital currency; it is a transformative movement with the potential to reshape the economic landscape for the African-American community. By offering an alternative to traditional financial systems, facilitating innovative economic models, and providing new pathways for investment and wealth creation, cryptocurrencies represent a significant step forward in the journey towards economic empowerment and autonomy.

Broader Implications of the Crypto Revolution

The crypto revolution extends far beyond the realm of finançe, with broader implications that permeate various aspects of society, particularly for the African-American community. This revolution, characterized by the rise of cryptocurrencies and blockchain technology, presents transformative possibilities not just in economic terms, but also in fostering social change, enhancing community connectivity, and redefining the concept of asset ownership and value.

One of the most profound impacts of the crypto revolution is its potential to level the playing field in financial inclusion. Traditional banking systems have often marginalized African-American communities through discriminatory practices and unequal access. Cryptocurrencies offer an alternative route, providing a decentralized financial system that operates independently of these entrenched biases. This democratization of financial access is not just about enabling transactions; it's about opening doors to economic participation and empowerment that have been historically closed to many in the African-American community.

Beyond mere financial transactions, blockchain technology, the backbone of cryptocurrencies, offers a new paradigm for trust and transparency in all manners of social and economic interactions. The immutable nature of blockchain can revolutionize how contracts, legal agreements, and public records are managed. For African-American communities, this means fairer and more transparent processes in areas such as property ownership, legal agreements, and even voting systems. Blockchain's ability to provide verifiable and immutable records can play a significant role in combating systemic issues such as voter suppression and property deed fraud, which have disproportionately affected African-Americans.

The crypto revolution also impacts the concept of asset ownership. Through tokenization, tangible and intangible assets can be digitized and fractionalized, making investment opportunities more accessible to a broader population. This shift can democratize investment in high-value assets like real estate or fine art, traditionally inaccessible to many

African-Americans due to high entry barriers. By fractionalizing these assets, individuals can own shares of physical or intellectual property, opening up new avenues for wealth creation and diversification.

Moreover, cryptocurrencies and blockchain technology enhance the global connectivity of the African-American community. They facilitate easier and more efficient cross-border transactions, enabling smoother financial interactions with the African continent and the global African diaspora. This connectivity can bolster economic ties, cultural exchange, and collective investment in international African-American initiatives, fostering a stronger sense of global community and shared economic goals.

However, the broader implications of the crypto revolution also encompass challenges such as the need for comprehensive education on digital finance, the volatility of cryptocurrency markets, and regulatory uncertainties. Navigating these challenges is crucial to fully harness the potential benefits of this revolution. It necessitates not just individual learning but also community-driven initiatives to spread knowledge, share best practices, and develop strategies to mitigate risks.

The crypto revolution offers far-reaching implications that go beyond digital currencies and financial transactions. It presents a transformative opportunity for the African-American community in terms of financial inclusion, social justice, asset ownership, and global connectivity. Embracing and understanding this revolution can lead to significant strides in economic empowerment and community advancement, marking a significant shift in the narrative of African-American participation in the global economy.

Exclusive Digital Realms: The Future of Ownership

The concept of ownership is being redefined in the digital age, moving beyond the traditional confines of physical possession to encompass exclusive digital realms. For the African-American community, this shift presents a unique opportunity to create, own, and control digital spaces and assets, marking a significant evolution in the understanding and exercise of ownership rights.

Exclusive digital realms, such as virtual property, digital art, and online platforms, offer new forms of asset ownership and investment. These realms are not bound by the physical limitations of the traditional market, allowing for greater flexibility, creativity, and accessibility. In the context of the African-American community, this opens up avenues for economic empowerment and cultural expression previously unavailable in physical markets.

One of the most prominent examples of these exclusive digital realms is the world of digital art and Non-Fungible Tokens (NFTs). NFTs represent a breakthrough in how art is created, sold, and owned, providing artists with a platform to monetize their work without going through traditional gatekeepers such as galleries or auction houses. For African-American artists, this means greater control over their work, direct profit from sales, and wider recognition in the global art market. Additionally, NFTs ensure authenticity and ownership, which is crucial in preserving the value and uniqueness of the artwork.

Another aspect of exclusive digital realms is the development of virtual real estate in digital environments or metaverses. These digital spaces allow users to create, buy, and sell virtual property, opening up a new market for real estate investment and development. For the African-American community, this presents a unique opportunity to invest in and develop virtual spaces that reflect their culture, interests, and aspirations. It also provides a platform for community building and social interaction within a digital environment, free from the constraints and biases of the physical world.

Moreover, the rise of exclusive digital realms has significant implications for intellectual property and digital rights. As more creative and economic activities move online, ensuring that African-American creators and entrepreneurs have full control and protection over their digital assets becomes increasingly important. This involves navigating complex issues around copyright, digital distribution, and revenue generation in the digital sphere.

The potential of exclusive digital realms extends to education and skill development as well. Digital platforms can offer tailored educational content, virtual training, and professional development opportunities, accessible to a wider audience. This democratization of education and skills training is key to ensuring that the African-American community can fully participate in and benefit from the digital economy.

However, the move towards exclusive digital realms also brings challenges, including the digital divide, the need for technological literacy, and potential market volatility. Addressing these challenges requires a combination of community effort, policy advocacy, and individual adaptability.

Exclusive digital realms represent the future of ownership, offering new opportunities for economic empowerment, cultural expression, and community building for African-Americans. Embracing these digital spaces and assets, while navigating their challenges, can lead to innovative pathways for growth and prosperity in the digital age.

Probing Deeper into Digital Ownership and Rights

In the rapidly evolving digital landscape, the concept of ownership and rights takes on new complexities and significance, particularly for the African-American community. As technology redefines how assets are created, shared, and managed, understanding and navigating digital ownership and rights become crucial in protecting interests and ensuring equitable participation in the digital economy.

Digital ownership in the context of intellectual property, such as digital art, music, writing, and software, is a critical area. With the rise of platforms for content creation and distribution, African-American creators have unprecedented opportunities to showcase their work and reach global audiences. However, this also poses challenges in protecting their intellectual property rights. Issues like copyright infringement and unauthorized use of digital work are prevalent, making it essential for creators to understand their rights and the mechanisms available for protection, such as digital watermarks, encryption, and legal frameworks.

Another significant aspect of digital ownership is related to data rights and privacy. In an age where personal data is a valuable commodity, safeguarding this data becomes paramount. African-

American users, like all digital users, must navigate issues related to data collection, usage, and sharing by digital platforms. Awareness and understanding of data rights, along with informed consent and robust privacy settings, are key to maintaining control over personal information.

Blockchain technology and smart contracts present revolutionary possibilities in managing digital ownership and rights. They offer a transparent, secure, and efficient way to establish and track ownership rights over digital assets, such as NFTs or virtual real estate. For the African-American community, this technology can provide a level of security and autonomy in digital transactions that was previously difficult to achieve. Smart contracts, in particular, enable automated, enforceable agreements that can protect the rights of all parties involved in digital transactions.

The concept of digital ownership also extends to online platforms and communities. African-American communities have the potential to create and manage their own digital spaces, fostering a sense of ownership and control over their digital presence. This can manifest in various forms, from social media groups and forums to digital marketplaces and networking platforms. These spaces not only serve as avenues for economic and social interaction but also as bastions of cultural expression and community solidarity.

However, delving into digital ownership and rights also reveals challenges, including the digital divide, which can limit access to technology and information about digital rights. Bridging this divide is crucial to ensure that the African-American community can fully participate in and benefit from the digital economy. Additionally, there is a need for ongoing education and advocacy to keep up with the rapidly changing digital landscape and its implications for ownership and rights.

Understanding and asserting digital ownership and rights are fundamental in the digital age, particularly for historically marginalized communities like African-Americans. Navigating these complex issues requires a combination of technological savvy, legal awareness, and proactive community engagement. By empowering themselves in these areas, African-Americans can protect their digital assets, maintain control over their personal data, and establish a strong and secure presence in the digital world.

The Role of Smart Contracts in Ownership

Smart contracts, a revolutionary aspect of blockchain technology, are redefining the concept of ownership in the digital age. These self-executing contracts with the terms of the agreement directly written into code offer a new level of transparency, security, and efficiency in managing digital assets. For the African-American community, smart contracts present an empowering tool to assert control over digital assets, streamline transactions, and protect intellectual property.

At their core, smart contracts are programs that automatically execute and enforce the terms of a contract when predetermined conditions are met. This automation eliminates the need for intermediaries, reducing the potential for disputes and errors. In the context of digital ownership, this means a more reliable and straightforward way of managing rights and transactions. For African-American creators and entrepreneurs, smart contracts provide a means to control how their work is used and monetized, ensuring they receive fair compensation and recognition.

One significant application of smart contracts is in the realm of digital art and NFTs (Non-Fungible Tokens). Artists can use smart contracts to define the terms of ownership and resale rights of their digital artwork. This includes embedding royalties into the contract, ensuring that the artist continues to receive a percentage of sales whenever their work is resold. This model not only provides ongoing income for the artist but also ensures the authenticity and scarcity of digital art, enhancing its value.

In addition to digital art, smart contracts have profound implications for other forms of digital ownership, such as music, literature, and software. Musicians, for instance, can use smart contracts to manage rights and royalties, offering a more direct and transparent way to earn revenue from their work. Similarly, authors and software developers can control the distribution and licensing of their digital products, safeguarding their intellectual property while reaching a wider audience.

Smart contracts also play a vital role in the emerging sector of decentralized finance (DeFi). They enable the creation of decentralized applications (dApps) that offer financial services such as lending, borrowing, and investing, without the need for traditional financial institutions. For the African-American community, DeFi can open up new opportunities for financial inclusion and investment, particularly for those who have been underserved by conventional banking systems.

Moreover, smart contracts can facilitate more efficient and secure transactions in real estate and business. They can be used to create transparent and enforceable agreements for property sales, business partnerships, and other commercial transactions. This can be particularly empowering for African-American entrepreneurs and investors, providing a level of security and trust in their business dealings.

However, the use of smart contracts also requires a thorough understanding of their legal implications and the technology itself. Ensuring that contracts are correctly coded and legally binding is crucial, as is educating community members about how to effectively use and benefit from this technology.

Smart contracts represent a transformative tool in the realm of digital ownership. By enabling more secure, transparent, and efficient management of assets and agreements, they offer significant opportunities for empowerment and economic advancement in the African-American community. As this technology continues to evolve, it holds the potential to significantly impact how ownership is defined and exercised in the digital world.

The Future of Digital Real Estate and Assets

The concept of digital real estate and assets is rapidly gaining momentum, marking a significant shift in the understanding and valuation of property and investments in the digital age. For the African-American community, this evolution offers unique opportunities for economic participation, wealth creation, and legacy building in virtual spaces.

Digital real estate refers to ownership of virtual land or properties in online environments, often within virtual worlds or metaverses. These properties, much like physical real estate, can be bought, sold, developed, and monetized. The future of digital real estate is promising, as these virtual spaces become venues for social interaction, commerce, education, and entertainment. For African-American investors and entrepreneurs, this presents an opportunity to enter a new market with potentially lower barriers to entry compared to traditional real estate. It also allows for creative expression and the development of culturally significant virtual spaces that reflect and celebrate African-American heritage and community.

In addition to virtual land, the concept of digital assets extends to various forms of online content, including digital art, music, and intellectual property, often tokenized using blockchain technology such as NFTs (Non-Fungible Tokens). The growing market for digital assets offers African-American creators a platform to showcase and monetize their work on a global scale, ensuring direct compensation and greater control over their intellectual property.

The future of digital assets also points toward the increasing use of cryptocurrencies as a form of investment and wealth storage. Cryptocurrencies offer an alternative to traditional financial systems, which have historically marginalized many in the African-American community. As these digital currencies gain acceptance and stability, they could become a significant part of investment portfolios, offering diversification and potentially high returns.

Furthermore, the burgeoning field of decentralized finance (DeFi) is set to redefine investment and asset management. DeFi platforms allow for a range of financial activities, from lending and borrowing to investing in decentralized assets, without the need for traditional banking institutions. This democratizes access to financial services, enabling African-American communities to engage in financial activities that were previously out of reach.

However, the digital real estate and assets market is not without its challenges. Issues such as market volatility, regulatory uncertainties, and the digital divide pose potential risks. Navigating these challenges requires education, strategic planning, and community support. It is crucial for the African-American community to stay informed about the latest developments in this space and to build networks that can provide guidance and support in these ventures.

The future of digital real estate and assets holds exciting possibilities for the African-American community. It offers new avenues for economic empowerment, creative expression, and community building in the digital realm. As technology continues to advance, these digital properties and assets are poised to become an increasingly important part of the economic landscape, offering novel ways for the community to invest, grow, and thrive in the digital age.

Chapter 4: Bridging Two Worlds: America and Africa

Slavery's Echo: Africa's Historical Legacy

The historical legacy of slavery casts a long shadow over the relationship between Africa and its diaspora, particularly African-Americans. This complex and painful history has profound implications, not just in a socio-cultural context but also in shaping economic and political dynamics between these two worlds. Understanding Africa's role in the transatlantic slave trade and its enduring echoes is crucial in forging a future of reconciliation, cooperation, and mutual growth.

Slavery, as a historical institution, was not solely a Western construct but involved significant participation by certain African states and traders. This involvement has left a deep-seated impact on the psyche and relations between African-Americans and their ancestral continent. For many African-Americans, there is a sense of loss, not just of ancestral homeland but also of culture, identity, and history. This loss is compounded by the complexity of feelings towards Africa – a mix of longing, betrayal, and a quest for roots and identity.

The legacy of slavery also manifests in economic disparities and underdevelopment in many African countries, partly due to the drain of human resources and the disruption of societal structures. This underdevelopment has implications for contemporary relationships, as it influences perceptions and interactions between Africans and the African-American diaspora. There is often a gap in understanding and expectations, with African-Americans and Africans viewing each other through the distorting lens of history and contemporary global politics.

However, this historical legacy also presents opportunities for healing and collaboration. The growing interest among African-Americans in exploring their roots and connecting with the African continent is a positive development. This reconnection can take various forms, from cultural exchanges and heritage tourism to more substantial engagements like business partnerships and investments in African economies. Such interactions not only foster a better understanding between African-Americans and Africans but also contribute to economic growth and development.

Moreover, the digital age offers new platforms for bridging the gap between Africa and its diaspora. Social media, online forums, and digital storytelling provide spaces for sharing histories, experiences, and perspectives. These digital connections can demystify and humanize both sides, breaking down stereotypes and building a foundation of empathy and understanding.

A critical aspect of bridging these two worlds is acknowledging and addressing the lingering effects of slavery. This involves education, open dialogue, and a concerted effort to understand the historical contexts and current realities of both African-Americans and Africans. Building these bridges requires not just a focus on economic and political ties but also a deep, mutual understanding and respect for each other's histories, struggles, and aspirations.

The echo of slavery in Africa's historical legacy is a profound element in the relationship between the continent and the African-American diaspora. While it poses challenges, it also opens up avenues for connection, understanding, and mutual support. By confronting this shared history honestly and empathetically, and leveraging the tools of the digital age, there is potential to transform this legacy into a foundation for a strong, cooperative future, enriching both Africa and its global diaspora.

Further Discussion on Africa's Role in Slavery

The role of Africa in the transatlantic slave trade is a complex and multifaceted aspect of history that necessitates a nuanced understanding. It's a narrative that intertwines with issues of coercion, economic compulsion, and the varied responses of African societies to European colonial powers. This deeper exploration into Africa's involvement provides a broader perspective on the historical events that shaped the African diaspora, particularly African-Americans.

Historically, the slave trade in Africa was not initially driven by external forces but existed within different societies for various purposes, including as a part of traditional tribal systems of servitude. However, with the advent of European colonization and the transatlantic slave trade, the scale and nature of slavery changed drastically. African kingdoms and traders became entangled in a larger global demand for labor, driven by the economic interests of European powers in their colonies, particularly in the Americas. This involvement varied significantly across the continent, with some African leaders actively resisting the trade, while others, driven by economic gain or political pressures, participated in and facilitated it.

Understanding this participation requires acknowledging the historical context in which African leaders and societies made these decisions. Many African societies were facing their own internal struggles, including conflicts with neighboring states. The introduction of European weaponry and goods further complicated these dynamics, often intensifying conflicts and leading to the capture and sale of prisoners of war into slavery. Additionally, the economic incentives offered by Europeans played a significant role in perpetuating the trade.

It is crucial to recognize the agency of African states and individuals in this history while also understanding the immense external pressures they faced. The role of European colonial powers in exploiting African societies, disrupting established economic and social systems, and imposing the brutal system of transatlantic slavery cannot be overstated. This complex interplay of internal and external factors contributed to the tragic narrative of the slave trade.

The legacy of Africa's role in slavery is still felt today, influencing the relationship between the continent and the African diaspora. For many African-Americans, this history is a source of pain and conflict, affecting their sense of identity and connection to Africa. Conversely, for Africans, there's often a struggle to reconcile this part of their history with the contemporary reality of Africa as a diverse and vibrant continent.

Furthermore, this history has broader implications for discussions about reparations, reconciliation, and historical accountability. It raises questions about how societies can confront and heal from such a traumatic past, and how descendants of both those who were enslaved and those involved in the trade can engage with this shared history.

Exploring further into Africa's role in slavery is essential for a comprehensive understanding of the transatlantic slave trade and its lasting impacts. It requires a balanced view that acknowledges the complexities of historical contexts, the varied roles of African states and societies, and the overarching influence of European colonialism. Understanding this history is a critical step in bridging the gap between Africa and its diaspora, fostering a dialogue based on truth, healing, and mutual respect.

Socioeconomic Unity: Breaking Internal Barriers

The journey towards socioeconomic unity between African-Americans and the African continent involves breaking down internal barriers that have historically impeded collaboration and mutual growth. These barriers are not just physical or geographical, but also encompass cultural, psychological, and economic dimensions. Addressing these challenges is crucial in forging a strong and productive relationship that benefits both African-Americans and Africans.

One of the primary internal barriers is the lack of knowledge and understanding about each other's current socio-economic realities. African-Americans may not be fully aware of the diverse cultural and economic landscapes of various African countries, just as Africans may have misconceptions about the life and struggles of African-Americans. Bridging this information gap is essential. This can be achieved through educational initiatives, cultural exchange programs, and media representation that accurately and comprehensively portray both African and African-American experiences.

Another significant barrier is the psychological impact of historical traumas, such as slavery and colonialism. These traumas have created a sense of mistrust and disconnection, hindering the establishment of a strong emotional and psychological bond. Healing these wounds requires open dialogues, shared cultural experiences, and collaborative efforts in acknowledging and addressing the past. This healing process is vital in building trust and empathy, laying the foundation for stronger socioeconomic ties.

Economic disparity and unequal access to resources also constitute major barriers. While African-Americans face systemic inequalities in the United States, many African countries grapple with challenges of poverty, underdevelopment, and the aftermath of colonial exploitation. Establishing socioeconomic unity involves collaborative efforts to address these disparities, including investment in education, infrastructure, and business development. Initiatives such as peer-to-peer investments, diaspora funds, and joint ventures can play a significant role in this regard.

The digital divide represents another barrier, as unequal access to technology limits the potential for collaboration and communication. Bridging this divide is crucial in the modern world, where digital connectivity is increasingly important for economic and social interaction. Efforts to improve digital infrastructure and accessibility in African communities, coupled with initiatives to enhance digital literacy among African-Americans, are key steps in this direction.

Cultural differences and biases can also hinder socioeconomic unity. Overcoming these requires a concerted effort to celebrate and respect each other's cultures. This can be facilitated through cultural festivals, exchange programs, and collaborative arts and media projects that showcase the richness and diversity of African and African-American cultures.

Achieving socioeconomic unity between African-Americans and the African continent requires a multi-faceted approach that addresses knowledge gaps, historical traumas, economic disparities, the digital divide, and cultural differences. By breaking down these internal barriers, a foundation can be laid for a relationship characterized by mutual understanding, respect, and shared goals. This unity has the potential to not only strengthen the economic and social fabric of both communities but also to create a powerful force for change and development on a global scale.

Economic Influence of African and African American Communities

African and African American communities play a pivotal role in the global economy. There are two major economic forces: the wealth of natural resources in Africa, particularly its significant gold reserves, and the substantial consumer spending power of African Americans in the United States. These factors are not merely elements of the global economy but are central to its functioning and growth. The potential of African technological innovation and the impact of African American culture and spending are seen as untapped reservoirs that could lead to substantial economic growth and development. This challenges the traditional view of these communities as peripheral to the global economy, instead positioning them as key drivers of economic change and innovation.

Continued Exploration of Socioeconomic Unity

Further exploring the concept of socioeconomic unity between African-Americans and Africa involves delving into collaborative strategies, shared challenges, and the potential for joint economic growth and social advancement. This exploration is not just about identifying common grounds but also about leveraging strengths and resources for mutual benefit and empowerment.

One key area for socioeconomic unity is in the realm of business and entrepreneurship. African-American entrepreneurs can explore opportunities to expand their businesses into African markets, tapping into the continent's burgeoning economies and growing consumer base. Conversely, African entrepreneurs can benefit from the established markets and business networks of African-Americans in the United States. Collaborative ventures, such as partnerships, joint ventures, or mentorship programs, can foster knowledge exchange, resource sharing, and market expansion.

Investment in technology and innovation presents another avenue for socioeconomic unity. Africa has a rapidly growing tech sector, with innovations in mobile technology, fintech, and e-commerce. African-Americans, particularly those in the tech industry, can play a pivotal role in this growth through investments, partnerships, and sharing of expertise. This collaboration can lead to the development of technological solutions tailored to the unique challenges and needs of both communities.

Education and skill development are critical for socioeconomic unity. Collaborative educational programs, such as student exchanges, online courses, and joint research initiatives, can enhance skills and knowledge transfer. These programs can focus on areas crucial for development, such as technology, entrepreneurship, healthcare, and sustainable development. By investing in education, both communities can build a skilled workforce that is better equipped to tackle the challenges of the modern economy.

Cultural exchange is also a significant component of socioeconomic unity. Understanding and appreciating each other's cultural heritage can strengthen bonds and create a more cohesive sense of identity. This can be achieved through cultural festivals, art exchanges, collaborative media projects, and tourism initiatives. Celebrating the rich cultural diversity of the African diaspora and the African continent can foster a sense of pride and solidarity, which is essential for unity.

Additionally, addressing shared social challenges is crucial. Both African-Americans and Africans face issues such as health disparities, environmental challenges, and social inequalities. Collaborative efforts to address these issues, such as joint health initiatives, environmental conservation projects, and social advocacy, can lead to improved outcomes for both communities. These joint efforts not only tackle immediate challenges but also build a foundation for long-term cooperation and mutual support.

The continued exploration of socioeconomic unity between African-Americans and Africa requires a comprehensive and collaborative approach. By focusing on areas such as business, technology, education, cultural exchange, and social challenges, meaningful connections can be forged that benefit both communities. This unity has the potential to create a powerful force for economic growth, social advancement, and cultural enrichment, transcending geographical boundaries and historical divides.

Collaborative Economic Strategies Between Continents

Establishing collaborative economic strategies between African-Americans and Africa is essential for mutual prosperity and development. These strategies hinge on creating synergistic relationships that leverage the unique strengths and resources of each continent. By working together, African-Americans and Africans can unlock new economic opportunities, foster innovation, and contribute to sustainable development in both regions.

One of the fundamental strategies is the promotion of direct investment. African-American investors can play a significant role in Africa's growth by investing in various sectors such as technology, agriculture, renewable energy, and infrastructure. These investments not only yield returns but also contribute to job creation and technological advancement in Africa. Conversely, African nations can explore investment opportunities in African-American businesses, supporting entrepreneurship and economic growth in the United States.

Another key strategy involves fostering trade relations. Building direct trade channels between African-American businesses and African markets can reduce dependency on traditional trade routes that often disadvantage both parties. This could involve setting up trade platforms, organizing trade missions, and establishing African-American/African trade associations. These efforts can enhance market access, improve the competitiveness of products, and strengthen economic ties.

Technology transfer and collaboration in innovation are also crucial. Collaborative projects in technology can address specific challenges such as healthcare, education, and financial inclusion. African-Americans can contribute their expertise in tech development and innovation, while Africans can provide insights into local contexts and needs. Such collaboration can result in innovative solutions that have a meaningful impact on both continents.

Partnerships in education and skill development are vital for long-term economic growth. Joint educational programs, research initiatives, and exchange programs can facilitate the sharing of knowledge and skills. These programs can focus on areas critical to economic development, such as entrepreneurship, digital literacy, and sustainable practices. By investing in human capital, African-Americans and Africans can build a workforce that is adaptable, skilled, and capable of driving economic growth.

Cultural and heritage tourism presents another opportunity for economic collaboration. Promoting tourism that celebrates the shared heritage of African-Americans and Africans can boost the tourism sector on both continents. This not only generates revenue but also fosters cultural exchange and understanding.

Lastly, collaborative efforts in addressing social and environmental challenges can have economic benefits. Joint initiatives in areas like healthcare, environmental conservation, and community development can lead to healthier, more sustainable communities, which are fundamental to economic prosperity. These initiatives can also open up opportunities for social entrepreneurship, where businesses are built around solving social problems.

Collaborative economic strategies between African-Americans and Africa are key to unlocking the potential of both continents. These strategies, encompassing investment, trade, technology, education, tourism, and social entrepreneurship, can create a strong foundation for sustainable growth and development. By working together and leveraging their respective strengths, African-Americans and Africans can build a prosperous and interconnected future.

Strengthening Ties for Economic Progress

The strengthening of ties between African-Americans and Africa for economic progress involves a multifaceted approach, focusing on collaboration, mutual understanding, and shared goals. This connection, rooted in a shared heritage and experiences, has the potential to drive significant economic growth and development on both continents.

One critical area for strengthening ties is the development of business networks and platforms that facilitate easy interaction and collaboration between African-American and African entrepreneurs. These platforms can serve as hubs for sharing business opportunities, resources, and market intelligence. By creating an integrated network, entrepreneurs and businesses can find partners for joint ventures, identify investment opportunities, and collaborate on projects that have mutual benefits.

Education and capacity building are also vital in strengthening these ties. Initiatives such as professional exchange programs, joint workshops, and seminars can help in sharing knowledge and best practices in various fields. This transfer of knowledge can be particularly beneficial in sectors where one group has more expertise than the other, ensuring that both African-Americans and Africans benefit from the latest advancements and innovations.

Investment in infrastructure development in Africa with the involvement of African-American expertise and capital can be a game-changer. Infrastructure projects in transportation, telecommunications, energy, and technology not only drive economic growth but also create jobs and improve the quality of life. African-American investors and companies can play a significant role in these projects, bringing in not just funds but also valuable expertise and technology.

Cultural exchange programs also play a crucial role in strengthening economic ties.

Understanding each other's cultures, histories, and societal structures is key to building trust and cooperation. Cultural exchanges, arts, and heritage programs can foster a deeper appreciation and respect, which is fundamental to successful business relationships.

Promoting trade between African-American communities in the U.S. and African countries is another key strategy. Reducing trade barriers, organizing trade fairs and expos, and creating awareness about products and services available on both sides can significantly boost trade. This includes supporting African-American businesses to navigate the African market and helping African businesses to understand and enter the American market.

Furthermore, leveraging technology for economic progress is essential. Collaborative technology projects, such as development of apps, software, or tech-based solutions to common problems, can be beneficial. African-Americans and Africans can collaborate on technological innovations that address specific challenges faced by communities on both continents, such as healthcare, education, or financial services.

Finally, a collaborative approach to addressing social challenges such as poverty, health disparities, and education can also strengthen economic ties. Joint initiatives in these areas not only contribute to social welfare but also create a stable and conducive environment for economic growth.

Strengthening ties between African-Americans and Africa for economic progress requires concerted efforts across various domains. By building strong networks, investing in education and infrastructure, promoting trade and cultural exchange, and leveraging technology, both communities can unlock immense economic potential and achieve shared prosperity. This collaboration, grounded in a mutual understanding and a shared past, holds the key to a more prosperous future for African-Americans and Africans alike.

Establishing New Economic Pathways

Creating new economic pathways between African-Americans and Africa is an endeavor that holds the promise of mutual benefit and strengthened bonds. These pathways are not just conduits of commerce and investment but also avenues for cultural exchange, knowledge transfer, and collaborative innovation. By establishing these connections, both African-Americans and Africans can tap into a wealth of resources and opportunities, fostering economic growth and development.

One essential pathway is the development of direct investment channels. African-American investors can identify opportunities in Africa's emerging markets, which offer potential for high returns. Investments can be directed toward sectors like technology, agriculture, renewable energy, and infrastructure, which are crucial for Africa's development. On the other hand, African investment in African-American businesses and ventures can also be encouraged, creating a two-way flow of capital and resources.

Another significant pathway is the creation of joint ventures and partnerships. These collaborations can harness the strengths of both African and African-American entrepreneurs, combining local knowledge with international expertise. Joint ventures in areas such as tech startups, manufacturing, and service industries can lead to innovative products and services, addressing market needs in both regions.

Leveraging technology for economic development is also key. Digital platforms can bridge geographical distances, allowing African and African-American entrepreneurs to collaborate, network, and conduct business. These platforms can host marketplaces for goods and services, provide resources and tools for business development, and offer spaces for virtual meetings and workshops.

Furthermore, the growth of e-commerce presents significant opportunities. African-American entrepreneurs can expand their market reach to Africa, where there's a growing consumer base with increasing purchasing power. Similarly, African entrepreneurs can access the American market, introducing unique products and tapping into a diverse consumer base. E-commerce platforms can also be used to promote products that reflect the cultural heritage and creativity of both communities.

Education and skill development are crucial pathways for long-term economic growth. Collaborative educational programs and exchanges can facilitate the sharing of knowledge and skills. These programs can focus on entrepreneurship, digital literacy, and other areas vital to the modern economy. By investing in human capital, African-Americans and Africans can build a workforce that is skilled, adaptable, and capable of driving economic growth.

Cultural and heritage tourism offers another pathway, providing economic opportunities while also fostering understanding and appreciation of each other's history and culture. Promoting tourism that explores the shared heritage of African-Americans and Africans can boost the tourism sector, generate revenue, and deepen cultural ties.

Finally, addressing shared social challenges can lead to economic benefits. Collaborative initiatives in healthcare, education, and environmental sustainability can improve the quality of life and create a stable environment for economic activities. These efforts can also open up opportunities for social entrepreneurship, where businesses address societal issues.

Establishing new economic pathways between African-Americans and Africa requires a comprehensive approach that encompasses investment, joint ventures, technology, e-commerce, education, tourism, and social entrepreneurship. By building these pathways, both communities can unlock new opportunities for growth, collaboration, and mutual understanding, paving the way for a prosperous and interconnected future.

The Future of African and African American Relations

Envisioning the future of relations between African-Americans and Africa requires a thoughtful consideration of the past, an understanding of the present, and a hopeful yet realistic outlook for the future. This relationship, steeped in a shared history yet marked by distinct experiences, holds immense potential for mutual growth, cultural exchange, and economic collaboration.

The future of this relationship will likely be characterized by increased connectivity, enabled by advancements in technology and communication. This digital interconnectedness can facilitate more profound cultural exchanges, educational collaborations, and business partnerships. African-Americans can play an integral role in the burgeoning tech industry in Africa, while African entrepreneurs can tap into the innovative spirit and market opportunities in the United States.

In terms of cultural and educational exchanges, the future will see more African-

Americans seeking to connect with their heritage and ancestry in Africa, leading to increased travel, study-abroad programs, and cultural projects. For Africans, this offers an opportunity to engage with the African-American experience, fostering a better understanding and appreciation of their diaspora counterparts. These exchanges will not only deepen mutual understanding but also enrich both cultures.

Economic collaboration will be a cornerstone of future relations. The potential for joint ventures in sectors like renewable energy, technology, agribusiness, and healthcare is vast. These collaborations can be facilitated by initiatives such as investment funds targeting African and African-American entrepreneurs, trade expos, and business incubators focused on nurturing startups from both communities.

The future also holds potential for collaborative efforts in addressing global challenges such as climate change, healthcare, and education. By pooling resources, knowledge, and expertise, African and African-American communities can develop innovative solutions to these challenges, benefiting not just their own communities but also contributing to global progress.

Furthermore, the arts and entertainment industries present a promising area for collaboration. African and African-American artists, musicians, filmmakers, and writers can work together to create works that reflect their shared heritage and individual experiences. This cultural output can not only be commercially successful but also play a crucial role in shaping global perceptions and narratives about people of African descent.

Addressing social and political challenges will also be a key aspect of future relations. Collaborative advocacy on issues such as racial justice, economic inequality, and political representation can lead to more effective strategies and impactful results. This collective action can be facilitated by global networks and organizations dedicated to African and African-American interests.

Finally, the future of African and African-American relations will hinge on the ability of both communities to confront and heal from the historical traumas of slavery and colonialism. This healing process is essential for building a foundation of trust and solidarity, paving the way for a relationship that is not defined by the pains of the past but inspired by the possibilities of the future.

The future of African and African-American relations is full of promise. It will be shaped by increased cultural, educational, and economic exchanges, collaborative efforts in addressing global challenges, and a shared commitment to healing and growth. By working together, African-Americans and

Africans can forge a path of shared prosperity, cultural richness, and global influence.

Chapter 5: Challenges on the Horizon

Prison Walls: Confronting Mass Incarceration

Mass incarceration in the United States represents a critical challenge that looms large on the horizon for the African-American community. This systemic issue, characterized by the disproportionate imprisonment of African-Americans, is a complex web of social, economic, and political factors that require urgent and comprehensive solutions.

The origins of mass incarceration can be traced back to policies and laws that disproportionately affect African-Americans, including the war on drugs and mandatory minimum sentencing laws. These policies have not only led to an increase in the prison population but have also perpetuated racial disparities within the criminal justice system. The impact of mass incarceration extends beyond the prison walls – it affects families, communities, and the overall social fabric of the African-American community.

One of the most immediate impacts is the disruption of family structures. Incarceration of a family member often leads to financial instability, emotional distress, and social stigma. Children of incarcerated parents face higher risks of poverty, poor academic performance, and emotional challenges. This disruption creates a cycle that can be difficult to break, perpetuating a legacy of disadvantage and marginalization.

Mass incarceration also has significant economic implications. It limits the economic potential of a substantial portion of the African-American community, as ex-offenders often face challenges in finding employment due to their criminal records. This barrier to re-entry contributes to a cycle of poverty and marginalization, hindering economic growth and stability not just for individuals, but for entire communities.

Moreover, the issue of mass incarceration is not just a matter of criminal justice but also of social justice. It reflects and exacerbates existing inequalities in society, including disparities in education, housing, and healthcare. Addressing mass incarceration requires tackling these underlying social issues, creating more equitable and inclusive systems that provide opportunities and support for all.

The challenge of mass incarceration also demands a reevaluation of the criminal justice system itself. This includes reforming sentencing laws, eliminating mandatory minimum sentences for non-violent offenses, and addressing the biases that exist at various levels of the judicial process. Restorative justice practices and rehabilitation programs should be prioritized over punitive measures, focusing on reintegration rather than retribution.

Community-based initiatives play a crucial role in addressing mass incarceration. These initiatives can provide support for families affected by incarceration, create educational and employment opportunities for ex-offenders, and advocate for policy changes. Building strong, supportive communities is key to creating an environment where individuals can thrive and contribute positively to society.

Confronting mass incarceration is a multifaceted challenge that requires a holistic approach. It involves addressing the systemic issues within the criminal justice system, tackling underlying social inequalities, and building strong, resilient communities. By taking comprehensive action, the African-American community can break the cycle of mass incarceration, creating a more just, equitable, and prosperous society.

Additional Perspectives on Mass Incarceration

Further examining mass incarceration reveals deeper layers of its impact on the African-American community and society as a whole. This system, often described as the new Jim Crow, extends its influence beyond the prison walls into various facets of life, shaping social dynamics, economic opportunities, and community well-being.

One critical aspect of mass incarceration is its historical context. The disproportionate incarceration of African-Americans can be traced back to the legacy of racial discrimination in the United States. This includes the Black Codes and Jim Crow laws post-Civil War, which criminalized many aspects of African-American life. The continuation of these discriminatory practices through modern policies underscores the systemic nature of the issue. Understanding this historical context is essential in comprehensively addressing the roots of mass incarceration.

The economic impact of mass incarceration extends beyond the individual level, affecting entire communities and the national economy. Incarcerated individuals are removed from the labor force, diminishing the economic productivity and potential of communities. Upon release, their prospects for employment are significantly hampered, contributing to cycles of poverty and economic marginalization. Additionally, the cost of maintaining the prison system places a significant burden on taxpayers, diverting resources from essential public services like education and healthcare.

Education is another area deeply impacted by mass incarceration. Schools in heavily policed communities, often with predominantly African-American populations, can resemble prisons, with metal detectors and police presence. This environment can create a school-to-prison pipeline, where disciplinary actions lead to interactions with the criminal justice system at a young age. The consequences of this pipeline are far-reaching, affecting educational outcomes and future opportunities for these students.

Mass incarceration also has profound health implications. Incarcerated individuals often face inadequate healthcare, and the stress and trauma of imprisonment can have long-term psychological effects. Additionally, the impact on families – including emotional stress and increased risk of poverty and health problems – contributes to a public health crisis that extends beyond the incarcerated individual.

The intersectionality of mass incarceration with other social issues is also notable. Issues such as housing, voting rights, and substance abuse are intricately linked with the criminal justice system. For instance, ex-offenders often face challenges in securing housing due to their criminal records, and many are disenfranchised, unable to vote even after serving their sentences. Addressing mass incarceration requires a holistic approach that considers these intersecting issues.

Community empowerment and advocacy are crucial in challenging the system of mass incarceration. Grassroots movements, community-led initiatives, and policy advocacy play pivotal roles in pushing for reform. These efforts can help shift the focus from punitive approaches to rehabilitative and restorative justice models, which emphasize healing and reintegration over punishment.

Mass incarceration is a multifaceted issue with far-reaching implications. It is a challenge that requires a nuanced understanding of its historical roots, systemic nature, and intersectionality with other social issues. Addressing this problem calls for comprehensive solutions that encompass policy reform, community empowerment, and a shift in societal attitudes towards justice and rehabilitation.

Green Gold: The Cannabis Dilemma

The legalization and commercialization of cannabis, often referred to as "Green Gold," present a complex dilemma with significant implications for the African-American community. This emerging industry holds tremendous economic potential but also raises critical issues of social justice, equity, and policy reform.

The legalization of cannabis in various states has opened up a booming industry. It promises job creation, significant tax revenues, and economic opportunities. For African-American entrepreneurs, this represents a chance to enter a lucrative new market. However, this opportunity is not without its challenges. The cannabis industry has high barriers to entry, including expensive licensing fees, complex regulations, and significant capital requirements, making it difficult for smaller, minority-owned businesses to compete.

Furthermore, the legalization of cannabis highlights issues of social justice, particularly considering the historical impact of marijuana criminalization on African-American communities. For decades, harsh drug laws have disproportionately targeted African-Americans, leading to high rates of incarceration for marijuana-related offenses. Even as cannabis becomes a legal and profitable industry, many African-Americans continue to suffer the long-term consequences of these convictions, including restricted access to housing, employment, and education.

One of the critical challenges in the cannabis dilemma is ensuring equity in the industry. This includes advocating for policies that provide opportunities for minority entrepreneurs, such as lower barriers to entry, access to funding, and support for small businesses. It also involves expunging past marijuana convictions and ensuring that those who were most impacted by criminalization have a fair chance to participate in and benefit from the industry.

Another aspect of the cannabis dilemma is the need for public education and responsible consumption. As the industry grows, there is a need to educate consumers about the safe and responsible use of cannabis products. This is particularly important in African-American communities, where there may be lingering stigma and misinformation about marijuana.

Additionally, the cannabis industry has the potential to contribute to medical and health advancements. With increasing recognition of the medicinal properties of cannabis, there is an opportunity for research and development in this area, potentially benefiting public health. African-American scientists and researchers can play a key role in this aspect of the industry, contributing to innovations that may have far-reaching health benefits.

Despite the increasing importance and profitability of these sectors, African Americans remain markedly underrepresented as leaders, founders, and owners. In technology, this is exemplified by the extremely low percentage of black-owned tech companies, highlighting a disparity in opportunities, funding, and representation. The cannabis industry presents a starker contrast: while the legal market for cannabis is burgeoning and profitable, African Americans, who have been disproportionately penalized in the era of cannabis prohibition, hold a negligible share in this industry. This raises critical questions about equity, justice, and access to economic opportunities in emerging and high-value sectors. It underscores the need for systemic change to address these disparities and ensure fair representation and participation of African Americans in these lucrative industries.

The cannabis dilemma represents both an opportunity and a challenge for the African-American community. Navigating this industry requires balancing economic potential with the need for social justice, equity, and community well-being. It calls for proactive policy advocacy, community engagement, and strategic entrepreneurship. By addressing these challenges head-on, the African-American community can potentially transform the narrative around cannabis, turning a history of criminalization into a future of opportunity and empowerment.

Further Examination of the Cannabis Industry

A deeper examination of the cannabis industry reveals a landscape fraught with complexities and opportunities, especially for the African-American community. As states continue to legalize cannabis, either for medicinal or recreational use, this burgeoning industry offers significant economic potential. However, it also raises questions about equity, social justice, and the rectification of past wrongs.

The economic promise of the cannabis industry is undeniable. With its legalization, there is a surge in demand for various cannabis products, leading to the growth of dispensaries, cultivation centers, and ancillary businesses. This growth can stimulate local economies, generate tax revenue, and create new job opportunities. For African-American entrepreneurs, this represents a chance to enter a market at its inception and potentially reap substantial rewards.

However, gaining access to this market is not straightforward. The legacy of marijuana criminalization heavily burdens the African-American community. Many individuals with past marijuana convictions, predominantly African-Americans due to racially biased enforcement of drug laws, find themselves excluded from participating in the legal cannabis market. This irony is stark: the same substance that led to mass incarceration of African-Americans is now a source of wealth and opportunity, but primarily for those outside these affected communities.

Addressing this issue requires legislative and policy reforms. States that have legalized cannabis are beginning to implement social equity programs aimed at enabling participation from those historically impacted by marijuana criminalization. These programs can include expunging criminal records related to cannabis, reducing entry barriers for starting cannabis businesses, and allocating a portion of cannabis business licenses to minority entrepreneurs. However, the effectiveness and implementation of these programs vary widely, and there is much room for improvement.

Furthermore, the cannabis industry poses challenges related to health and public safety. While cannabis is praised for its medicinal benefits, like pain relief and control of certain forms of epilepsy, there is also the potential for abuse and health risks, particularly among young people. The industry and communities must navigate these health considerations, ensuring that public education and responsible usage are prioritized.

Another dimension is the potential impact on the workforce. With the legalization of cannabis, issues such as workplace drug policies and employee rights come into focus. Businesses and policymakers must balance safety and fairness, considering the changing legal status of cannabis and its presence in the workforce.

Finally, the cannabis industry offers opportunities for research and development. There is still much to learn about the plant's medicinal properties, potential uses, and effects. African-American scientists and researchers can play a significant role in this new frontier of research, contributing to a body of knowledge that could have significant health and economic benefits.

The cannabis industry, while promising as a new economic frontier, is laden with challenges that need careful navigation. For the African-American community, these challenges include overcoming barriers to entry, addressing the lingering effects of past criminalization, ensuring health and public safety, and participating in the ongoing research and development in the field. Addressing these issues thoughtfully and effectively can transform the cannabis industry into a source of economic empowerment and social justice.

Red Lines on a Map: The Lasting Scars of Redlining

Redlining, a discriminatory practice that began in the 1930s, continues to leave lasting scars on the African-American community. This practice involved outlining areas with significant African-American populations in red ink on maps as a warning to mortgage lenders, effectively denying Black people access to housing loans and opportunities. The consequences of redlining are profound and multi-generational, affecting community wealth, access to education, and overall quality of life.

The impact of redlining extends beyond just housing discrimination. It set the stage for systemic economic and social disparities. Neighborhoods that were redlined have historically been underinvested in, leading to a lack of resources such as quality schools, healthcare facilities, and public services. This underinvestment perpetuates a cycle of poverty and limits opportunities for residents, impacting their economic mobility and future prospects.

Redlining also contributed to the racial wealth gap. Homeownership is a primary means of building wealth in the United States. By denying African-Americans the opportunity to own homes and accumulate wealth, redlining has had a lasting impact on the economic stability of Black families. The effects are still felt today, with African-American homeownership rates significantly lower than their white counterparts, and home values in historically redlined neighborhoods remaining substantially lower.

Furthermore, the practice of redlining has led to urban decay and blight in many African-American neighborhoods. The lack of investment and economic opportunities has resulted in deteriorating infrastructure, abandoned properties, and a decline in public safety. These conditions not only affect the quality of life of residents but also discourage new investments, perpetuating a cycle of neglect.

Redlining also has significant health implications. Neighborhoods affected by redlining often lack access to healthy food options, green spaces, and medical facilities. This lack of resources contributes to higher rates of health problems among residents, including asthma, diabetes, and heart disease. The stress associated with living in under-resourced and neglected neighborhoods can also have psychological impacts, affecting mental health and overall well-being.

Combating the legacy of redlining requires comprehensive policies and targeted investments. This includes efforts to increase homeownership among African-Americans, such as providing access to affordable mortgages, down payment assistance, and homeowner education programs. Reinvestment in historically redlined neighborhoods is also crucial, focusing on improving infrastructure, public services, and economic development.

Additionally, there is a need for educational reform and investment in these communities. Ensuring access to quality education can help break the cycle of poverty and provide residents with better opportunities. This should be coupled with health and wellness initiatives to address the disparities caused by years of neglect.

Redlining has left deep and enduring scars on the African-American community. Its legacy is evident in the economic, social, and health disparities that persist today. Addressing this legacy requires a multi-faceted approach that tackles not only the symptoms but also the root causes of these disparities. By acknowledging and actively working to repair the damage caused by redlining, there is potential to foster more equitable and thriving communities.

Analyzing the Continued Impact of Redlining

The insidious practice of redlining, despite being officially outlawed, continues to exert a profound impact on African-American communities. This systemic denial of financial services and housing opportunities has long-lasting effects that ripple through generations, contributing to disparities in wealth, health, and overall community well-being.

The economic repercussions of redlining are still starkly evident. African-American communities that were once redlined face significant challenges in accumulating wealth. The denial of home loans and the devaluation of property in these neighborhoods have led to a substantial wealth gap between white and African-American families. Homeownership is a key asset in most American families' portfolios, and the lack of this asset in African-American families translates into a reduced ability to pass wealth down to subsequent generations, perpetuating cycles of poverty.

Redlining has also contributed to spatial segregation that continues to affect urban landscapes. African-American communities often remain isolated from economic opportunities, quality education, and essential services. This segregation not only limits access to resources but also perpetuates stereotypes and social stigma, further entrenching racial divides.

The health disparities arising from redlined communities are significant and multifaceted. Limited access to healthcare facilities, coupled with environmental factors such as poor housing conditions and pollution, result in higher incidences of chronic illnesses among residents. Mental health is also impacted by the stresses associated with living in under-resourced neighborhoods, including exposure to crime and lack of green spaces.

Education in redlined communities often suffers due to a lack of funding and resources. Schools in these neighborhoods typically receive lower funding due to the lower property taxes collected, leading to overcrowded classrooms, outdated materials, and fewer educational programs. This educational inequality hampers the ability of children in these communities to compete academically and professionally in the future.

The ongoing impact of redlining also extends to community development and infrastructure. Neighborhoods that were redlined are often marked by neglected infrastructure, limited public transportation, and a lack of investment in community amenities. This neglect not only affects the quality of life of residents but also discourages new investments and economic growth in these areas.

Addressing the continued impact of redlining requires comprehensive and targeted interventions. This includes policies that promote fair lending practices, investment in affordable housing, and revitalization of neglected neighborhoods. It also calls for initiatives to improve education and healthcare access in these communities.

Efforts to rectify the damages of redlining must also involve a broader societal commitment to acknowledging and addressing systemic racism. This involves reexamining how city planning, economic policies, and social services are implemented to ensure they do not perpetuate the inequalities rooted in redlining.

The continued impact of redlining is a stark reminder of how past discriminatory practices can have enduring effects. It underscores the need for deliberate and sustained efforts to address these inequalities, not just through policy changes but also through a collective commitment to fostering more equitable and inclusive communities.

Guardians or Oppressors? Policing the Black Community

The relationship between law enforcement and the African-American community has long been fraught with tension, mistrust, and conflict. This complex dynamic poses one of the most pressing challenges on the horizon, raising fundamental questions about the role of policing and the broader criminal justice system in African-American communities.

Historically, the police have been seen by many in the African-American community not as protectors but as enforcers of discriminatory laws and practices. This perception is rooted in a history of systemic racism, from the enforcement of segregation laws to the more recent war on drugs, which disproportionately targeted African-Americans.

Instances of police brutality, racial profiling, and the over-policing of African-American neighborhoods have further exacerbated this trust deficit.

The consequences of this fraught relationship are profound. It not only undermines the fundamental role of police in ensuring public safety but also perpetuates a cycle of fear, resentment, and resistance within the community. This dynamic hampers effective law enforcement and leaves genuine public safety needs unmet. Moreover, it contributes to the criminalization of African-American youth, perpetuating stereotypes and exposing them to the criminal justice system at an early age.

Addressing these challenges requires a multi-dimensional approach. Firstly, there's a need for significant police reform. This includes training in implicit bias, de-escalation techniques, and community policing practices that emphasize building relationships and trust within the community. Greater accountability measures, such as independent oversight boards and body cameras, are also crucial in ensuring transparency and accountability in police actions.

Community engagement is another key aspect of reforming the relationship between police and African-American communities. This involves creating platforms for dialogue and collaboration, where community members can voice their concerns, and police can provide insights into their work. Building these bridges can foster mutual understanding and respect, laying the groundwork for a more cooperative and constructive relationship.

Another important factor is addressing the underlying social issues that contribute to crime and conflict. This includes investing in education, job opportunities, mental health services, and other social services that can alleviate the conditions that often lead to criminal behavior. By addressing these root causes, the need for heavy policing can be reduced, leading to a more preventative approach to public safety.

The role of the broader criminal justice system cannot be overlooked. Reforms in sentencing laws, bail practices, and prison conditions are crucial in ensuring that the system is fair, just, and rehabilitative rather than punitive. This also involves addressing the disproportionate representation of African-Americans in the prison system and tackling the biases that lead to this disparity.

Transforming the relationship between law enforcement and the African-American community is a critical challenge that requires concerted efforts from all sides. It involves not just reforming policing practices but also addressing the broader systemic issues that contribute to this complex dynamic. By working towards a more equitable, just, and cooperative relationship, the goal of ensuring public safety and fostering a healthy, thriving community can be achieved.

Rethinking Policing in the Context of Black Communities

Rethinking the approach to policing in African-American communities is a crucial challenge, requiring a profound shift in strategies, policies, and perspectives. The relationship between law enforcement and these communities has been marked by historical tensions and systemic issues, necessitating a re-evaluation of how policing is conducted to ensure it aligns with the principles of justice, equity, and community welfare.

One of the primary steps in rethinking policing is adopting a community-oriented approach. This approach emphasizes building trust and partnerships between police officers and community members. It involves officers being present in the community not just as enforcers of the law but as active participants in community life, understanding and addressing the unique challenges these communities face. This can be achieved through regular community meetings, involvement in local events, and collaboration with community leaders and organizations.

Another critical aspect is the reform of policing practices. This includes the implementation of bias training to address conscious and unconscious racial prejudices among law enforcement officers. De-escalation training is also vital, equipping officers with skills to resolve situations peacefully and reduce the likelihood of violence. Additionally, the adoption of policies that prioritize non-lethal methods and emphasize the sanctity of life is crucial in changing how police interactions are handled.

The accountability of police officers and departments is paramount in rethinking policing. This involves not only clear and transparent protocols for handling instances of misconduct but also systems that allow for community oversight. Independent review boards and transparent investigations into police actions can help build trust and ensure that officers are held accountable for their actions.

There is also a need to address the over-policing of African-American communities. This requires a critical examination of practices such as racial profiling and stop-and-frisk policies, which disproportionately target these communities. Reducing the over-policing and instead focusing on addressing the root causes of crime, such as poverty, lack of education, and unemployment, can lead to more effective and just outcomes.

Furthermore, the concept of public safety must be expanded beyond traditional policing. Investing in social services such as mental health care, housing, education, and community development can address many of the underlying issues that lead to crime. This approach, often referred to as "defunding the police," does not necessarily mean abolishing police departments but reallocating some resources towards these vital community services.

In conclusion, rethinking policing in the context of African-American communities is a multifaceted challenge that involves a paradigm shift in law enforcement strategies and policies. It requires a move towards community-oriented policing, reform of policing practices, accountability, a reduction in over-policing, and a broader approach to public safety. Addressing this challenge is crucial for building a more equitable and just society, where the police are seen not as oppressors but as partners in fostering safe and thriving communities.

Chapter 6: Seizing Digital Opportunities

A Continent's Collaboration: Africa and African Americans

The digital age presents unprecedented opportunities for collaboration between Africa and the African-American community. This collaboration, harnessing the power of technology, has the potential to create significant economic, social, and cultural benefits for both continents. By connecting through digital platforms, these two groups can share resources, knowledge, and experiences, fostering a mutually beneficial relationship.

One significant area of collaboration is in the field of technology and innovation. African countries have seen a surge in tech startups and digital entrepreneurship, while the African-American community in the U.S. has a growing number of tech professionals and innovators. By collaborating on tech projects, sharing expertise, and investing in joint ventures, they can drive technological advancements that address specific challenges relevant to both communities. This can include developing apps for financial inclusion, health technology solutions, and educational platforms.

Another vital area for collaboration is in business and commerce. E-commerce platforms can open up new markets for African and African-American products, allowing artisans, entrepreneurs, and businesses to reach a global audience. This digital trade not only boosts economic growth but also promotes cultural exchange by allowing each community to experience the other's products and services.

Education and skill development are also crucial areas for collaboration. Online learning platforms can be used to share educational resources, conduct joint research, and provide training in critical skills needed in today's economy. This can help in closing the skills gap in Africa and provide African-American professionals opportunities to engage in mentorship and knowledge exchange.

The digital realm also offers a space for cultural exchange and understanding. Through digital media, art, and storytelling, African and African-American creators can collaborate on projects that explore their shared heritage and experiences. This exchange not only enriches the cultural tapestry of both communities but also fosters a deeper understanding and appreciation of their respective histories and current realities.

Collaboration in healthcare through telemedicine and digital health initiatives is another area with significant potential. Leveraging digital platforms, African-American health professionals can contribute to healthcare delivery in African countries, where there may be a shortage of medical professionals. This can include remote consultations, sharing of medical knowledge, and collaboration in health research.

Furthermore, digital platforms can be instrumental in advocacy and social change. By uniting their voices on issues such as racial justice, economic inequality, and political representation, African and African-American communities can amplify their impact on the global stage. Social media campaigns, online forums, and digital conferences can facilitate this collective advocacy, enabling coordinated action on shared concerns.

The collaboration between Africa and the African-American community in the digital age holds immense potential. By leveraging digital technologies for innovation, commerce, education, cultural exchange, healthcare, and advocacy, these communities can strengthen their ties, share in each other's growth, and make significant strides in addressing common challenges. This digital collaboration is not just about economic or technological gains; it's about building a connected and empowered global African diaspora.

Enhancing Collaboration Through Digital Means

In an era where digital technology has become a cornerstone of daily life, leveraging these tools to enhance collaboration between African-Americans and Africa offers a pathway to substantial progress and innovation. Digital platforms and tools provide the means to bridge geographic distances, foster direct communication, and create shared spaces for collaborative efforts.

One of the primary ways digital technology can enhance collaboration is through the establishment of virtual networks and platforms. These digital spaces can serve as hubs for African and African-American entrepreneurs, activists, educators, and artists to connect, share ideas, and launch collaborative projects. For instance, online business incubators and accelerators can offer mentorship, resources, and networking opportunities, driving innovation and growth in both communities.

E-commerce and digital marketplaces represent another area ripe for collaboration. By leveraging these platforms, artisans, manufacturers, and entrepreneurs from Africa and the African-American community can access new markets and customer bases. This not only drives economic growth but also promotes cultural exchange, as products unique to each culture are shared globally.

In the field of education, digital platforms can facilitate knowledge exchange and learning opportunities. Online courses, webinars, and virtual exchange programs can provide valuable educational experiences, accessible to a wide audience. Collaborative educational initiatives can focus on areas such as cultural studies, history, business, technology, and other fields that foster a deeper understanding and connection between the two communities.

Digital technology also offers a powerful tool for social and political activism. Social media campaigns, online petitions, and virtual forums can bring attention to issues affecting African and African-American communities, mobilizing global support and action. These platforms can also be used to share stories and experiences, building a narrative that reflects the diverse perspectives and realities of these communities.

Healthcare is another sector where digital collaboration can have a significant impact. Telemedicine initiatives can allow African-American healthcare professionals to provide consultation and support to patients and fellow professionals in Africa. Collaborative research projects can also be conducted more efficiently through digital communication and data-sharing tools.

Cultural collaboration is also enhanced through digital means. Collaborative art projects, virtual cultural festivals, and online galleries can showcase the rich heritage and creativity of both communities. These initiatives not only celebrate cultural diversity but also provide a source of economic opportunity for artists and cultural practitioners.

Finally, digital collaboration can play a crucial role in addressing environmental challenges. Shared digital platforms can facilitate the exchange of ideas and best practices in areas such as sustainable agriculture, renewable energy, and conservation efforts, combining traditional knowledge with modern technology to find solutions to environmental issues.

Enhancing collaboration between African-Americans and Africa through digital means offers a plethora of opportunities for growth, innovation, and mutual understanding. By harnessing the power of digital technology, these communities can create new avenues for economic prosperity, educational enrichment, cultural exchange, and social activism, paving the way for a more interconnected and collaborative future.

Digital Alchemy: From Tangible to Intangible Assets

The transformation of assets from tangible to intangible forms, a process akin to alchemy in the digital age, is redefining value creation and economic participation. This shift towards intangible assets, including digital content, intellectual property, and online platforms, presents unique opportunities and challenges, particularly for the African-American community.

In this digital alchemy, intellectual property (IP) emerges as a crucial asset. For African-American creators – be it musicians, writers, artists, or entrepreneurs – the digital landscape provides a platform to protect, manage, and monetize their IP. Tools like blockchain for securing digital rights, online marketplaces for selling digital art, and platforms for streaming music and literature allow creators to reach global audiences while retaining control over their work.

The rise of digital content as a valuable asset is another facet of this transformation. The ability to create and distribute content digitally – from videos and podcasts to blogs and digital art – opens up new avenues for creativity and entrepreneurship. African-American content creators can harness these platforms not just for economic gain but also for cultural expression and influence, shaping narratives and sharing experiences that resonate globally.

Social media platforms and online networks have become vital intangible assets. They provide spaces for marketing, community building, and influence. For African-American businesses and influencers, these platforms offer a way to build a brand, engage with audiences, and drive both social and economic value.

Another aspect of digital alchemy is the transformation of services into digital formats, such as online consulting, virtual events, and e-learning. These services expand the reach and accessibility of businesses, educators, and professionals, enabling them to connect with clients and audiences far beyond their physical location.

The digitization of assets also extends to the realm of finance. Cryptocurrencies and digital tokens represent a new form of asset that transcends traditional banking systems. For African-Americans, this offers an alternative means of investment and wealth accumulation, particularly for those who have been underserved by conventional financial institutions.

However, the shift to intangible assets is not without challenges. It requires digital literacy and access to technology – areas where the digital divide still exists. Ensuring equitable access to digital tools and resources is crucial for the African-American community to fully participate in and benefit from this transformation.

Moreover, the intangible nature of these assets raises issues around security, privacy, and ownership. Navigating these challenges requires understanding digital rights, leveraging protective technologies, and staying informed about the evolving digital landscape.

The transformation from tangible to intangible assets in the digital age – digital alchemy – offers significant opportunities for economic innovation, cultural expression, and wealth creation. For the African-American community, this shift presents a chance to redefine value and success in the digital economy. However, maximizing these opportunities requires overcoming challenges related to access, literacy, and security, ensuring that the benefits of digital alchemy are accessible and equitable.

The Transformation of Asset Ownership in the Digital Age

The digital age has revolutionized the concept of asset ownership, shifting the focus from physical possessions to digital assets that include data, digital content, and online platforms. This transformation has significant implications for African-American communities, offering new opportunities for wealth creation, cultural expression, and economic empowerment.

Digital assets, such as social media profiles, websites, digital art, and online businesses, have become increasingly valuable. These assets provide not only potential financial returns but also opportunities for personal branding, community engagement, and influence. For African-American entrepreneurs and creators, this means leveraging digital platforms to build businesses, promote art and ideas, and connect with audiences and customers worldwide.

One of the key aspects of this transformation is the monetization of digital content. Content creators – including writers, artists, and videographers – can now reach global audiences through platforms like YouTube, Instagram, and personal blogs. This democratization of content production and distribution enables African-American creators to bypass traditional gatekeepers in media and entertainment, offering a direct route to monetization and audience engagement.

Another significant development is the rise of cryptocurrencies and blockchain technology. These innovations provide new ways of owning and transferring value, independent of traditional banking systems. For African-American communities, often underserved by conventional financial institutions, cryptocurrencies can offer an alternative for wealth accumulation and investment. Additionally, blockchain technology offers unique advantages in terms of transparency and security, particularly for protecting intellectual property and managing digital contracts.

The digital transformation also extends to the concept of ownership in the sharing economy. Platforms like Airbnb and Uber have redefined what it means to own assets like housing and vehicles, turning them into potential sources of income. This sharing economy can provide African-American communities with flexible economic opportunities, utilizing assets in new and innovative ways.

However, the shift to digital asset ownership brings challenges, particularly regarding access and equity. The digital divide – disparities in access to technology and the internet – can limit the ability of some in the African-American community to participate fully in the digital economy. Addressing this divide is crucial for ensuring that these transformative opportunities are accessible to all.

Protecting digital assets is another challenge. Issues like data privacy, cybersecurity, and intellectual property rights are central in the digital realm. Navigating these issues requires awareness and understanding of digital rights and access to tools and resources for protecting online assets.

The transformation of asset ownership in the digital age opens up a world of possibilities for African-American communities. It provides new avenues for wealth creation, self-expression, and economic empowerment. However, realizing the full potential of this transformation requires addressing challenges related to access, equity, and asset protection. By navigating these challenges, African-American communities can harness the opportunities of the digital age to build a more prosperous and empowered future.

Collective Wealth: The Smart Contract Revolution

The advent of smart contracts, powered by blockchain technology, heralds a revolution in the way collective wealth can be managed and grown, especially for the African-American community. Smart contracts, with their inherent transparency, security, and efficiency, offer a transformative approach to handling agreements and transactions in the digital world.

Smart contracts are self-executing contracts with the terms directly written into code. They run on blockchain technology, ensuring that the contract is carried out exactly as programmed without the need for intermediaries. This technology has significant implications for collective wealth management, as it opens up new avenues for investment, fundraising, and asset management that are more accessible, equitable, and secure.

One of the key applications of smart contracts in collective wealth building is in the realm of investments. African-American communities can leverage these contracts to create investment pools or funds that are more transparent and democratic. Members of the community can invest in shared ventures, with the terms and profit distributions being managed automatically and transparently by the smart contract. This approach reduces the potential for mismanagement or fraud, ensuring that every participant receives their fair share of the returns.

Smart contracts also offer new possibilities in crowdfunding and community-based financing. Projects or ventures that benefit the community, such as local businesses, social programs, or real estate developments, can be funded collectively through smart contracts. This method not only ensures transparency in how the funds are used but also allows contributors to see exactly how their investment is making an impact.

Another application is in the domain of asset and property management. Smart contracts can be used to manage communal assets, such as community centers, shared workspaces, or rental properties. These contracts can automate various aspects of management, from rent collection to maintenance scheduling, making the process more efficient and reducing the burden on individual community members.

Smart contracts also have the potential to revolutionize the way intellectual property and creative works are monetized. African-American artists, musicians, and creators can use smart contracts to manage the rights and royalties of their work. This system ensures they are compensated fairly and promptly for every use of their work, whether it's a song played on the radio or a piece of digital art sold online.

However, the adoption of smart contracts and blockchain technology also presents challenges, including the need for technical knowledge and understanding of how these systems work. There is a need for education and resources to ensure that members of the African-American community can effectively utilize these technologies for wealth building.

The smart contract revolution offers a powerful tool for collective wealth management and growth within the African-American community. By providing a means for transparent, secure, and efficient management of investments, assets, and intellectual property, smart contracts can help build a more financially empowered and prosperous community. However, realizing this potential requires overcoming technical barriers and ensuring broad access to the necessary tools and knowledge.

The Growing Influence of Smart Contracts

The rise of smart contracts is reshaping the landscape of digital transactions and agreements, signaling a significant shift in how business is conducted and assets are managed. This technology, built on blockchain platforms, is not just a tool for tech enthusiasts but a revolutionary development with far-reaching implications, particularly for communities historically marginalized in traditional economic systems, like African-Americans.

Smart contracts are essentially programs that automatically execute and enforce the terms of a contract once predetermined conditions are met. Their growing influence is evident in several key areas:

Democratization of Finance

Smart contracts are at the heart of decentralized finance (DeFi) movements, which aim to create an open, accessible financial system. For African-American communities, this presents an opportunity to bypass traditional financial institutions that have often been inaccessible or biased. DeFi can offer more equitable access to financial services like loans, investments, and insurance.

Real Estate and Property Management

In the real estate sector, smart contracts can revolutionize property transactions by automating various processes, including sales, leases, and rentals. This automation reduces the need for intermediaries, lowering transaction costs and making real estate more accessible to a broader range of people, including those in African-American communities.

Social Finance Concept

The concept of Social Finance is envisioned as a transformative approach to financial engagement, drawing a parallel to the impact of social media on communication and interaction. It proposes a new way of understanding and participating in financial activities, where the emphasis is on community and collaborative investment, rather than individual or purely profit-driven motives. This approach could involve community-based investment projects, socially responsible investing, and platforms that allow for collective financial decisions and support. By doing so, Social Finance aims to democratize finance, making it more accessible and aligned with social goals and community needs. It's about creating a financial ecosystem that values social impact as much as economic returns, encouraging a shift from traditional, isolated financial transactions to a more integrated, socially-conscious approach.

Intellectual Property and Royalties

For artists, musicians, and writers within the
African-American community, smart contracts
provide a way to ensure they are fairly compensated
for their work. By automating royalty payments,
creators can receive their dues instantly and
transparently whenever their work is used.

Supply Chain Transparency

Smart contracts offer transparency in supply
chains, ensuring that products are sourced and
produced ethically. This is particularly relevant for
African-American consumers and businesses
increasingly concerned with ethical consumption and
corporate responsibility.

Voting and Governance

In community organizations and governance,
smart contracts can be used to create transparent and
tamper-proof voting systems. This can empower
African-American communities in decision-making
processes, ensuring that their voices are heard and
counted in a secure manner.

Legal and Contractual Agreements

Smart contracts can simplify legal processes
by automating contract execution, reducing the time
and cost associated with legal agreements. This
automation can be particularly beneficial for small

businesses and entrepreneurs in the African-American community, who often face barriers in accessing legal services.

Challenges and Considerations

Despite their potential, smart contracts also pose challenges. There is a learning curve associated with understanding and utilizing blockchain technology. Ensuring that African-American communities have access to education and resources to leverage this technology is crucial. Additionally, regulatory frameworks for smart contracts are still evolving, requiring careful navigation.

The growing influence of smart contracts represents a significant opportunity for African-American communities to engage in more equitable financial practices, protect intellectual property, and participate in transparent and efficient digital transactions. As this technology continues to evolve, it holds the potential to significantly alter the economic landscape, providing new avenues for empowerment and wealth creation. However, maximizing these benefits will require overcoming educational, technological, and regulatory challenges.

Investing in the Digital Economy

Investing in the digital economy is an essential strategy for the African-American community to harness the immense potential of technological advancements. The digital economy, characterized by its rapid growth and constant innovation, offers diverse opportunities for wealth creation, entrepreneurship, and economic empowerment.

E-Commerce and Online Marketplaces

The rise of e-commerce presents significant opportunities for African-American entrepreneurs. Online marketplaces have lowered barriers to entry for starting a business, allowing entrepreneurs to reach a global customer base with relatively low startup costs. Investing in e-commerce platforms, either as a seller or as a platform developer, can yield substantial returns. Additionally, these platforms can serve as a showcase for unique products that reflect African-American culture and creativity.

Tech Startups and Innovation

The technology sector continues to be a major driver of economic growth. Investing in tech startups, particularly those that offer solutions to unique challenges faced by the African-American community, can be both profitable and impactful. This can include health tech, educational software, financial technology, and more. African-American investors can also play a crucial role in providing capital and mentorship to budding African-American tech entrepreneurs.

Economic Redirection and New World Order

This theme deals with a radical proposal to redirect the substantial spending power of African Americans to create a 'black virtual utopia.' It is based on the idea that a strategic and temporary redirection of spending – for a period of 6 months to a year – could have a transformative impact on the global economy. The concept involves African Americans consciously choosing to circulate their financial resources within their own communities, thereby building a strong, self-reliant economic base. This strategy is seen as a way to challenge and potentially reshape the current economic order, creating a more equitable and just economic system. It also touches upon the broader theme of a new world order, where knowledge and economic participation are central to power dynamics. The fear is that those who are disconnected from this new order – the 'have-nots' – will be left significantly disadvantaged, while the 'haves' who adapt and engage will accumulate wealth and influence. This point calls for a proactive approach to ensure economic inclusion and equity, particularly within the black community, to prevent further economic stratification.

Digital Content Creation

The digital economy has democratized content creation, allowing individuals to generate income through platforms such as YouTube, Instagram, and TikTok. African-American content creators can leverage these platforms to monetize their creativity, whether through advertising, sponsorships, or selling digital products and services. This not only provides a source of income but also amplifies diverse voices and stories.

Cryptocurrency and Blockchain

While cryptocurrencies and blockchain technology are relatively new and come with risks, they also offer unique investment opportunities. African-Americans can invest in cryptocurrencies as a means of diversifying their investment portfolio. Additionally, blockchain technology offers opportunities beyond cryptocurrencies, including in areas like supply chain management, digital identity, and secure transactions.

Remote Work and Digital Services

The shift towards remote work has opened up new possibilities in the digital services sector. African-Americans can invest in developing digital skills and services, such as coding, graphic design, digital marketing, and virtual assistance. These skills can be marketed globally, providing access to a broader range of job opportunities and income streams.

Cybersecurity

As the digital economy grows, so does the importance of cybersecurity. Investing in cybersecurity companies or developing skills in this area can be highly beneficial. Cybersecurity is a critical component of all digital businesses, and expertise in this field is in high demand.

Challenges and Risks

Investing in the digital economy also involves navigating various challenges and risks. This includes staying abreast of technological changes, understanding the regulatory landscape, and managing the inherent risks associated with digital investments, such as market volatility and cybersecurity threats.

The digital economy offers a wealth of opportunities for the African-American community to build wealth, foster entrepreneurship, and participate in the burgeoning global digital marketplace. By strategically investing in various sectors of the digital economy, from e-commerce to tech startups and digital content creation, African-Americans can tap into new sources of income and economic growth. However, success in this arena requires staying informed, continuously learning, and carefully managing risks.

The Future of Digital Investments and Collaborations

The future of digital investments and collaborations holds immense promise, especially for African-American communities looking to expand their economic horizons and influence. As the world increasingly moves towards a digital-first economy, the potential for innovative investments and collaborative ventures in the digital space is vast and varied.

Expanding Digital Entrepreneurship

The future will see a continued rise in digital entrepreneurship, with more African-Americans launching online businesses, apps, and digital platforms. These ventures can range from e-commerce and digital marketing to tech solutions addressing specific community needs. Collaborations between African-American entrepreneurs and African tech innovators can lead to the development of products and services with global appeal and relevance.

Investment in Emerging Technologies

Technologies like artificial intelligence (AI), machine learning, and the Internet of Things (IoT) are reshaping industries. Investing in these technologies, either directly or through venture capital funds, can provide high growth potential. Collaborations in research and development between African-American tech professionals and African educational institutions can also drive innovation in these areas.

Leveraging Blockchain for Social Good

Blockchain technology has applications far beyond cryptocurrencies. In the future, we can expect to see its use in enhancing transparency in charitable donations, ensuring ethical supply chains, and even in voting systems. Collaborations that leverage blockchain for social impact projects can be particularly beneficial for African-American and African communities.

Growth of Digital Content and Media

The demand for diverse digital content and media will continue to grow. Investing in digital media platforms that cater to or are run by African-Americans can not only be profitable but also ensure representation and give a voice to the community. Collaborations in film, music, and digital art can create new cultural narratives and open up international markets.

Fintech and Financial Inclusion

The fintech sector will be crucial in addressing financial inclusion, an area of significant importance for historically underserved communities. Digital banking, peer-to-peer lending platforms, and mobile payment solutions can offer more accessible financial services. Collaborative ventures in fintech can bridge gaps between African-American consumers, businesses, and the banking sector.

Digital Education and Skill Development

As technology continues to evolve, so does the need for continuous learning and skill development. Investing in digital education platforms and collaborating on educational content can provide widespread access to learning resources. This is crucial for empowering African-American communities with the skills needed in a digital economy.

Challenges and Considerations

While the future is bright, it is not without challenges. Ensuring equitable access to technology, protecting against digital divide issues, and maintaining privacy and security in digital transactions are crucial considerations. Collaborative efforts will need to focus on not just creating opportunities but also addressing these challenges head-on.

The future of digital investments and collaborations is ripe with opportunities for economic growth, social impact, and community empowerment. By strategically engaging in these digital ventures, African-American communities can play a pivotal role in shaping the digital economy and ensuring it serves the needs and interests of diverse populations.

The Role of NFTs in Economic Empowerment

Non-Fungible Tokens (NFTs) have emerged as a novel and powerful tool in the realm of digital assets, offering unique opportunities for economic empowerment, particularly for African-American artists, creators, and entrepreneurs. NFTs, digital tokens that represent ownership of a unique item or piece of content on the blockchain, are transforming the way we think about art, collectibles, and digital ownership.

NFTs enable artists and creators to monetize their work in new ways. For African-American artists, who have historically faced barriers in accessing traditional art markets, NFTs offer a direct route to global audiences. Artists can sell their digital art, music, or other creative works as NFTs, ensuring they retain a significant portion of the profits. Moreover, smart contracts associated with NFTs can allow creators to receive royalties automatically every time their work is resold.

NFTs provide a secure way to prove the authenticity and ownership history of digital assets. This is particularly valuable in the art world, where provenance and originality are paramount. African-

American artists can use NFTs to establish and maintain the authenticity of their work, enhancing its value and their reputation.

NFTs also offer new ways for creators to engage with their audience and build communities. Artists can create limited edition NFTs, exclusive digital experiences, or special access to events, fostering a closer connection with their fans. This community-building aspect can be particularly empowering for African-American creators looking to establish a supportive and engaged audience.

The NFT market provides an alternative investment opportunity for individuals who might not have access to traditional art or investment markets. African-American investors can purchase, trade, and collect NFTs, diversifying their investment portfolio. Additionally, as the market for NFTs grows, it can offer financial gains to those who invest wisely.

While NFTs offer significant opportunities, they also come with challenges. The market can be volatile, and the value of NFTs can fluctuate widely. There are also environmental concerns regarding the energy consumption of blockchain technology. Navigating these challenges requires a careful and informed approach to investing in and creating NFTs.

To maximize the benefits of NFTs, educational initiatives are necessary to inform African-American communities about how to create, buy, and sell NFTs. Understanding the technology, the market dynamics, and the legal aspects of NFTs is crucial for artists, creators, and investors to make informed decisions.

NFTs represent a significant shift in the digital economy, offering new avenues for economic empowerment, especially for African-American creators and entrepreneurs. By providing a platform for monetizing creative work, ensuring authenticity, building communities, and offering investment opportunities, NFTs have the potential to play a vital role in economic empowerment. However, realizing their full potential requires education, awareness, and a cautious approach to navigate the risks and challenges in this evolving market.

Expanding Access to Digital Wealth

In an era where the digital economy is rapidly expanding, ensuring broad access to digital wealth becomes crucial, especially for communities that have historically faced economic disparities, like African-Americans. Digital wealth, encompassing assets ranging from cryptocurrencies and NFTs to online businesses and digital real estate, offers new avenues for economic growth and empowerment. Expanding access to these opportunities is key to achieving financial equity and inclusion.

Fundamental to expanding access to digital wealth is enhancing digital literacy. Education initiatives focusing on understanding the digital economy, from e-commerce and digital marketing to blockchain technology and digital asset management, are essential. These programs can empower individuals with the knowledge and skills needed to navigate and capitalize on digital opportunities effectively.

Access to technology and high-speed internet is a prerequisite for participating in the digital economy. Addressing the digital divide, which disproportionately affects African-American communities, is crucial. This involves not only improving infrastructure but also making technology more affordable and accessible to these communities.

Encouraging and supporting digital entrepreneurship can provide a pathway to creating digital wealth. This can be achieved through incubators, accelerators, and funding programs that specifically target African-American entrepreneurs. These resources can help in starting and scaling online businesses, developing apps, or creating digital content.

Financial technology (fintech) can play a significant role in expanding access to digital wealth. Investing in fintech startups that focus on serving underbanked or unbanked populations can facilitate greater financial inclusion, allowing more individuals to participate in the digital economy.

Platforms that democratize investment, allowing individuals to invest in stocks, digital assets, or crowdfunding ventures with minimal capital, can help expand access to digital wealth. Educating communities about these platforms and the associated risks is key to ensuring informed and responsible investment decisions.

Simplifying the process of buying, selling, and managing digital assets like cryptocurrencies and NFTs can make these assets more accessible. This involves creating user-friendly platforms and providing educational resources to help individuals understand and navigate these markets.

Advocating for policies that promote digital inclusion and fair regulation of digital markets is essential. This includes lobbying for policies that protect online consumers, support digital entrepreneurs, and ensure equitable access to digital services and assets.

Grassroots initiatives and community-based programs can play a pivotal role in expanding access to digital wealth. These initiatives can provide localized training, resources, and support for community members looking to explore digital opportunities.

Expanding access to digital wealth in the African-American community requires a multifaceted approach, addressing educational, infrastructural, entrepreneurial, and regulatory barriers. By focusing on these areas, it's possible to not only increase participation in the digital economy but also to ensure that the benefits of this rapidly growing economic sector are equitably distributed. This expanded access can lead to greater financial empowerment and a narrowing of the wealth gap for historically underserved communities.

Chapter 7: Summarizing the Journey from Historical Ideologies to Future Prospects

The journey from historical ideologies that have shaped the African-American experience to the prospects of a decentralized, digital future is both a reflection of resilience and a roadmap for empowerment. This journey underscores the evolution from a past marked by struggles against oppression and inequality, to a future where technology offers new avenues for economic and social liberation.

Historically, African-American ideologies have been deeply influenced by the fight for civil rights, equality, and justice. Figures like Martin Luther King Jr., Malcolm X, and W.E.B. Du Bois laid down foundational philosophies emphasizing non-violence, economic empowerment, self-reliance, and the dual consciousness of African-Americans. These ideologies were born out of the necessity to combat systemic racism, segregation, and economic disparities.

Fast forward to the present, the African-American community faces a new set of challenges and opportunities in the digital age. The rise of the internet and digital technologies has democratized access to information, created new economic opportunities, and provided platforms for cultural expression and global connectivity. However, this digital revolution also presents challenges such as the digital divide, online discrimination, and the need for digital literacy and cybersecurity.

Looking towards a decentralized future, there is immense potential for African-Americans to harness digital technologies for economic growth and social change. Blockchain technology and cryptocurrencies offer opportunities for financial inclusion and empowerment, particularly for those who have been marginalized by traditional financial systems. Digital platforms provide avenues for African-American entrepreneurs and artists to reach global markets and audiences, breaking down barriers that have historically limited access to economic opportunities and cultural exchange.

Moreover, the decentralization of information and resources in the digital age aligns with the historical ideologies of self-reliance and empowerment. It offers a pathway to more equitable and participatory systems, where African-Americans have greater control over their economic and cultural narratives. This decentralized future also presents opportunities for community building, advocacy, and collaboration, both within the African-American community and between Africa and its diaspora.

The transition from historical ideologies to future prospects in a digital world is not just a shift in tools and technologies but a transformation in mindset and approach. It involves embracing innovation while staying grounded in the values and struggles that have defined the African-American experience. It requires balancing the opportunities presented by digital technologies with the need to address ongoing issues of inequality, access, and representation.

The journey of the African-American community, from historical ideologies to a future of decentralized opportunities, is marked by resilience, adaptability, and a continuous pursuit of empowerment and justice. By leveraging the tools and possibilities of the digital age, while remaining anchored in the rich heritage and collective struggles of the past, the African-American community can chart a course towards a more prosperous, equitable, and empowered future.

Chapter 8: Conclusion: Envisioning a Decentralized Destiny

The Importance of a Unified Approach to Economic Empowerment

In the journey toward a decentralized destiny, the importance of a unified approach to economic empowerment stands out as a crucial element for the African-American community. This unity is not just about collective action but also about harnessing diverse perspectives, skills, and resources to build a strong, resilient economic foundation that benefits all members of the community.

The concept of unity in economic empowerment is deeply rooted in African-American history. From the collective struggles during the Civil Rights Movement to the collaborative spirit of the Black Wall Street, unity has always been a powerful tool for overcoming adversity and achieving communal goals. In today's digital age, this unified approach takes on new dimensions and possibilities.

A unified approach allows for the pooling of resources, knowledge, and networks. This collective strength is particularly important in overcoming systemic barriers that have historically hindered African-American economic progress. By working together, the community can achieve greater scale, influence, and impact than individual efforts alone.

In the rapidly evolving digital economy, continuous learning and skill adaptation are key. A unified approach fosters an environment of shared learning, where knowledge about new technologies, market trends, and investment strategies can be disseminated throughout the community, empowering a wider audience to seize digital opportunities.

The decentralized nature of the digital economy offers an opportunity to create more inclusive economic systems. A unified approach ensures that these systems are designed to be equitable, addressing the needs of the most marginalized within the community. This includes advocating for fair policies, creating accessible platforms, and ensuring that the benefits of technology are widely distributed.

Entrepreneurship is a critical driver of economic empowerment. A unified approach in supporting African-American entrepreneurs can lead to more successful ventures. This support can come in various forms, including mentorship, funding, networking opportunities, and collaborative projects that bring together different talents and ideas.

Economic empowerment is closely linked to community resilience. A unified approach to economic development helps build communities that can withstand economic downturns and systemic challenges. This involves not just financial investments but also developing social infrastructure, such as education, healthcare, and community services.

Finally, a unified approach is essential in advocating for systemic change. The African-American community faces unique challenges that require collective advocacy to address. This includes fighting for policy changes, challenging discriminatory practices, and promoting equity and justice in economic systems.

In conclusion, a unified approach to economic empowerment is vital for realizing a decentralized destiny. It harnesses the collective strength, fosters shared learning, creates inclusive systems, supports entrepreneurship, builds community resilience, and advocates for systemic change. As the African-American community navigates the digital age, this unified approach will be key to seizing new opportunities and overcoming persistent challenges, paving the way for a future that is economically empowered and equitable.

The Call to Action for the Black Community

As we envision a future defined by decentralized opportunities and equitable growth, there emerges a clear call to action for the African-American community. This call is not just a directive but a rallying cry to embrace the potential of the digital age, confront persisting challenges, and actively shape a destiny that reflects the community's aspirations and values.

The first call to action is to actively engage with the digital revolution. This means acquiring digital literacy, understanding emerging technologies like blockchain and AI, and leveraging these tools to create economic opportunities. The community must encourage its youth to pursue careers in STEM fields, ensuring future generations are well-equipped to thrive in a digital world.

Economic empowerment must be a collective goal. This involves supporting African-American businesses, encouraging entrepreneurship, and creating investment opportunities within the community. The focus should be on building wealth that can be sustained and passed down through generations, helping to close the racial wealth gap.

Education is the cornerstone of empowerment. The community must advocate for equitable access to quality education and invest in resources and programs that provide lifelong learning opportunities.

This education should not only cover traditional subjects but also teach financial literacy and entrepreneurial skills.

In the pursuit of a decentralized destiny, solidarity within the community is paramount. This means supporting each other's endeavors, sharing knowledge and resources, and standing united in the face of social and economic challenges. It also involves building strong networks that can provide support, mentorship, and guidance.

The African-American community must continue to be at the forefront of the fight for social justice and equity. This involves challenging systemic racism, advocating for policy changes, and participating in civic processes. It's crucial to not only address the symptoms of inequality but also tackle its root causes.

The African-American community should strengthen its connections with the African continent and the global African diaspora. These connections can open up new avenues for cultural exchange, economic collaboration, and shared advocacy on global issues.

The well-being of the community is essential. There should be a focus on improving access to healthcare, promoting mental health, and addressing environmental and social determinants of health that disproportionately affect African-Americans.

Lastly, the community must continue to celebrate and preserve its rich cultural heritage. This involves not only understanding the past but also creating new cultural narratives that reflect the diversity and dynamism of the African-American experience.

In conclusion, the call to action for the African-American community in envisioning a decentralized destiny is multifaceted and profound. It encompasses embracing technology, economic empowerment, education, community solidarity, social justice, global connectivity, health, and cultural heritage. By responding to this call, the community can build a future that is not only prosperous and equitable but also reflective of its rich history and aspirations.

Reflecting on the Potential of a New Nation within a Nation

The concept of a new nation within a nation, particularly for the African-American community, is a powerful reflection of self-determination and empowerment in the modern world. This idea encompasses creating a self-sustaining, self-governing community that thrives within the larger national context, leveraging the collective strength, culture, and aspirations of African-Americans.

The cornerstone of this new nation within a nation is economic self-sufficiency. This involves building a robust economic ecosystem where African-American businesses are supported, community-based financial institutions thrive, and local economies flourish. It's about creating and circulating wealth within the community, ensuring that economic benefits uplift all members.

Central to this vision is the preservation and celebration of African-American culture. By nurturing cultural institutions, supporting artists and creators, and investing in cultural education, the community can maintain a strong sense of identity and heritage. This cultural autonomy is not just about looking inward but also sharing the richness of African-American culture with the wider world.

Education is pivotal in realizing the potential of a new nation within a nation. This includes not only formal education but also community education that addresses the specific needs and history of African-Americans. Investing in educational programs that emphasize STEM, financial literacy, history, and civic engagement can equip future generations with the tools to succeed and lead.

Effective political representation and advocacy are vital for ensuring the interests of this new nation are recognized and addressed. This involves active participation in the political process, from voting to holding public office, and advocating for policies that advance the well-being of the African-American community.

Prioritizing health and wellness is essential for a thriving community. This means addressing health disparities, investing in healthcare infrastructure, and promoting practices that enhance physical, mental, and emotional well-being. A healthy community is more capable of achieving its full potential.

The strength of this new nation lies in its unity and mutual support. It's about fostering a sense of community where members support each other, share resources, and work together towards common goals. This solidarity is the foundation upon which economic, cultural, and educational aspirations are built.

While focusing on building a strong internal community, it's also crucial to maintain global connections. This involves engaging with the African diaspora, building international partnerships, and participating in global discussions. These connections enrich the community's perspective and offer opportunities for collaboration and growth.

In conclusion, the potential of creating a new nation within a nation for African-Americans is vast and multi-dimensional. It encompasses economic independence, cultural preservation, educational empowerment, political advocacy, health and wellness, community solidarity, and global connectivity. By striving towards this vision, the African-American community can create a future that is not only prosperous and self-sustaining but also deeply rooted in its rich heritage and collective strength.

Affiliations and Partnerships

"40'aces": An App's Role in Revolution

"40'aces," an innovative app developed as part of a broader vision for economic empowerment and community transformation, stands at the forefront of a technological revolution for the African-American community. This app embodies the aspiration to create a decentralized ecosystem where African-Americans can achieve economic independence, access educational resources, and build a tightly-knit community of support and growth.

1. Economic Empowerment Platform

At its core, "40'aces" is designed to be a robust platform for economic empowerment. It facilitates a marketplace where users can buy and sell products and services within the African-American community, thereby keeping the economic benefits within the community. This aspect of the app encourages entrepreneurship and supports local businesses, creating a cycle of wealth that uplifts all members.

2. Investment and Financial Education

A key feature of "40'aces" is its focus on investments and financial education. The app provides tools and resources for users to learn about financial management, investment strategies, and wealth-building principles. It also offers a platform for community-based investments, allowing users to collectively fund and support promising ventures and projects.

3. Cultural Exchange and Preservation

"40'aces" serves as a digital space for cultural exchange and preservation. It allows users to explore and share African-American history, art, music, and literature, thereby fostering a strong sense of identity and pride. This feature ensures that the app is not just a tool for economic activity but also a hub for cultural enrichment.

4. Community Building and Networking

The app is designed to foster community building and networking. It provides forums and chat features where users can connect, share experiences, and offer support. Whether for business advice, mentorship, or social connection, "40'aces" is a space where the African-American community can come together in solidarity and collaboration.

5. Promoting Health and Wellness

Recognizing the importance of health and wellness, "40'aces" includes features related to healthcare information, wellness tips, and access to health resources. This component of the app addresses the need for accessible health and wellness education within the community.

6. Advocacy and Social Justice

"40'aces" also plays a role in advocacy and social justice. It provides a platform for users to engage with social issues, participate in advocacy campaigns, and stay informed about matters affecting the African-American community. This feature underscores the app's commitment to not just economic growth but also social progress and justice.

7. Technological Innovation and Accessibility

The app's design focuses on user-friendliness and accessibility, ensuring that it is inclusive and easy to navigate for all users, regardless of their technological proficiency. Regular updates and innovations are planned to keep the app relevant and effective in meeting the evolving needs of the community.

In conclusion, "40'aces" is more than just an app; it is a revolutionary tool that encapsulates the aspirations for economic empowerment, cultural richness, community solidarity, and social justice within the African-American community. By harnessing technology, "40'aces" aims to create a decentralized platform that empowers, educates, and unites, paving the way for a prosperous and self-sustaining future.

"WeCannBe": Narratives and Enterprises Reimagined

"WeCannBe," short for "With Equity Create a New Narrative for Black Enterprise," is a pioneering initiative that embodies a transformative vision for African-American entrepreneurship and narrative. This company, conceived by the author, stands as a beacon for innovation, empowerment, and change, actively reimagining the way narratives and enterprises are shaped within the African-American community.

1. Empowering African-American Entrepreneurs

At its heart, "WeCannBe" is focused on empowering African-American entrepreneurs. This involves not only providing financial resources and investment but also offering mentorship, networking opportunities, and strategic guidance. The company recognizes that access to capital is just one part of the equation; equally important is the know-how to navigate the business world effectively.

2. Reframing Narratives

"WeCannBe" is dedicated to reframing the narratives around African-American entrepreneurship. By highlighting success stories, showcasing innovative business models, and providing platforms for entrepreneurs to share their journeys, the company aims to inspire and motivate. It seeks to challenge stereotypes and change perceptions, showing the world the creativity, resilience, and excellence of African-American business owners.

3. Fostering Community Collaboration

Understanding the power of community, "WeCannBe" emphasizes collaboration over competition. The company encourages partnerships among African-American businesses, fostering an ecosystem where enterprises support one another. This collaboration extends to joint ventures, shared marketing efforts, and collective advocacy for better business conditions.

4. Innovation and Technology

"WeCannBe" places a strong emphasis on leveraging technology and innovation. The company supports tech-driven business ideas and helps entrepreneurs integrate the latest technologies into their operations. From e-commerce platforms to digital marketing strategies, "WeCannBe" is at the forefront of bringing technological advancements into African-American enterprises.

5. Educational Initiatives

Recognizing the importance of education, "WeCannBe" invests in educational programs and workshops. These initiatives cover various aspects of business, including financial literacy, marketing, legal aspects of entrepreneurship, and leadership skills. The aim is to equip entrepreneurs with the knowledge and skills they need to succeed.

6. Social Impact and Responsibility

"WeCannBe" is deeply committed to social impact and corporate responsibility. The company encourages and supports businesses that not only seek profit but also contribute positively to their communities. This includes ventures focusing on social issues, environmental sustainability, and community development.

7. Expanding Access and Opportunities

Lastly, "WeCannBe" is dedicated to expanding access and opportunities for African-American entrepreneurs. This means breaking down barriers that have traditionally impeded access to markets, resources, and networks. The company works to create pathways for underrepresented entrepreneurs, ensuring that the business landscape is diverse and inclusive.

In conclusion, "WeCannBe" is more than a company; it is a movement towards a new narrative in African-American enterprise. It stands for equity, empowerment, and excellence, actively working to reshape the landscape of entrepreneurship. Through its efforts, "WeCannBe" aims to create a future where African-American businesses are thriving, innovative, and impactful, contributing to a more equitable and prosperous society.

Glossary

1. Black Dollar: The economic power and influence of the Black community in the United States.

2. Martin's Dream: Refers to Martin Luther King Jr.'s vision for economic justice as a cornerstone of civil rights.

3. Garvey's Vision: The ideology of Marcus Garvey, emphasizing self-reliance and independence for the Black community.

4. Malcolm's Assertion: The economic empowerment and restitution ideals advocated by Malcolm X.

5. Du Bois's Duality: W.E.B. Du Bois's concept of "double consciousness," the sense of two identities experienced by African Americans.

6. Digital Age: The era marked by the widespread adoption of digital technology and its impact on society.

7. Legacy of the Panthers: The lasting influence of the Black Panthers, a Black revolutionary organization of the 1960s.

8. Desegregation: The process of ending racial segregation, particularly in schools and public spaces.

9. Re-envisioning the Black Wall Street: A reimagination of the historic Black Wall Street, a prosperous Black community in Tulsa, Oklahoma, before the 1921 Tulsa Race Massacre.

10. Crypto Revolution: The transformational changes brought about by cryptocurrencies like Bitcoin and blockchain technology.

11. Smart Contracts: Self-executing contracts with the terms of the agreement directly written into code.

12. NFTs (Non-Fungible Tokens): Unique digital assets that represent ownership of a specific item or piece of content.

13. Mass Incarceration: The high rates of imprisonment in the United States, disproportionately affecting Black communities.

14. Cannabis Dilemma: The challenges and opportunities surrounding the legalization and regulation of cannabis.

15. Redlining: The discriminatory practice of denying services or opportunities to specific neighborhoods, particularly based on racial composition.

16. Digital Real Estate: Ownership of digital spaces or assets within virtual environments.

17. Africa's Historical Legacy: The impact of Africa's history, including slavery, on the African diaspora.

18. Socioeconomic Unity: The goal of achieving economic and social cohesion within the Black community.

19. Collaborative Economic Strategies: Cooperative efforts between Africa and African Americans to enhance economic opportunities.

20. Guardians or Oppressors: A reflection on the role of law enforcement in Black communities and the need for reform.

21. Asset Ownership in the Digital Age: The evolving nature of ownership in the context of digital assets and technology.

22. 40'aces: An app designed to digitally reunite communities and promote economic empowerment.

23. WeCannBe: A company dedicated to reimagining Black enterprises and narratives.

24. Unified Approach: The idea of working together as a united community to achieve common goals.

25. Call to Action: A rallying cry for individuals and communities to take concrete steps toward empowerment.

26. New Nation within a Nation: The concept of a self-sustaining and empowered Black community coexisting within the larger nation.

27. Affiliations and Partnerships: Collaborative relationships and alliances that promote economic empowerment.

28. Decentralized Destiny: Envisioning a future where economic power is distributed and accessible to all.

29. Age of the Black Dollar: The era characterized by the economic growth and influence of the Black community.

Made in the USA
Columbia, SC
02 October 2024

42909219R00111